•Barthol

Cycling
in the
Cotswolds

Bartholomew

An imprint of HarperCollins*Publishers*

Published by Bartholomew
An imprint of HarperCollins*Publishers*
77-85 Fulham Palace Road
London W6 8JB

First published 1997
© Bartholomew 1997

Routes compiled by Sheila Booth and
Marion and Maurice Teal
Designed by Creative Matters Design Consultancy, Glasgow

Photographs reproduced by kind permission of the following:
Bourton Model Village page 43; J. Allan Cash pages 26, 29, 35; International Photobank
pages 24, 59; Bill Meadows Picture Library pages 16, 94; The National Trust
Photographic Library pages 39, 45, 56, 67; Maurice and Marion Teal pages
19, 32, 36, 47, 48, 55, 71, 75, 102, 103; Andy Williams pages 5, 8, 11.

The landscape is changing all the time. While every care has
been taken in the preparation of this guide, the Publisher accepts
no responsibility whatsoever for any loss, damage, injury or
inconvenience sustained or caused as a result of using this guide.

Printed in Hong Kong

ISBN 0 7028 3513 7
97/1/16

CONTENTS

KEY TO ROUTES

Route		Grade	Distance km (miles)		Time to allow	Page
1	Bourton-on-the-Water and the Slaughters	moderate	15	(9.5)	1-4 hours	14
2	Kemble and the Cotswold Water Park	easy	16.5	(10.5)	1-3 hours	17
3	Sherborne Brook and the River Windrush	moderate	18.5	(11.5)	1-3 hours	20
4	Bibury – Arlington Row and the Trout Farm	moderate	19	(12)	1-3 hours	22
5	Burford, Swinbrook and the Barringtons	moderate	23.5	(14.5)	2-3 hours	25
6	Tetbury, Chavenage House and Cherington	easy	24.5	(15)	2-4 hours	28
7	The Dunt Valley and its churches	moderate	30	(18.5)	2-4 hours	31
8	Moreton-in-Marsh and Chipping Campden loop	moderate	30.5	(19)	2-3 hours	34
9	Painswick and the northern Stroudwater valleys	strenuous	32.5	(20)	3-4 hours	38
10	Bourton, the Barringtons and the Rissingtons	moderate	33.5	(21)	2-3 hours	42
11	Eastern Cotswolds – Filkins, Fairford and Eastleaches	moderate	36.5	(23)	2-4 hours	46
12	Sudeley Castle, Guiting Power and Stanway House	moderate	37	(23)	2-4 hours	50
13	The southern end – Lansdown, Dyrham and Batheaston	strenuous	43.5	(27)	3-5 hours	54
14	Stow-on-the-Wold, Bourton, Windrush and Bledington	strenuous	46	(28.5)	3-4 hours	58
15	Cirencester, Chedworth, Northleach and Barnsley	moderate	47	(29)	3-6 hours	62
16	Chipping Campden and Cotswold gardens	strenuous	57	(35.5)	4 hours	66
17	Tetbury to Castle Combe – South Cotswold villages	moderate	61	(38)	4-6 hours	70
18	Moreton-in-Marsh to the Rollright Stones	moderate	62.5	(39)	4-5 hours	74
19	Tetbury and the Frome Valley	strenuous	63	(39)	5-6 hours	78
20	Southern Cotswold edge – Nailsworth loop	strenuous	69.5	(43)	5-7 hours	82
21	Northern Cotswold edge – Winchcombe loop	moderate	73	(45.5)	5-7 hours	86
22	Northleach, Naunton, Broadwell and Bledington	strenuous	74	(46)	4-7 hours	90
23	Kemble, Elkstone and the Coln Valley	strenuous	76.5	(48)	5-8 hours	95
24	South west Cotswolds – Stroud loop	strenuous	80.5	(50)	5-7 hours	100
25	The Cotswolds – a grande randonnée	strenuous	100	(62.5)	6-10 hours	106

Distances have been rounded up or down to the nearest 0.5km (mile).

Route colour coding

undemanding rides compiled specifically with families in mind
15-25km (10-15 miles)

middle distance rides suitable for all cyclists
25-40km (15-25 miles)

half-day rides for the more experienced and adventurous cyclist
40-60km (25-40 miles)

challenging full-day rides
over 60km (over 40 miles)

grande randonnée – a grand cycling tour
100km (60 miles)

 Routes marked with this symbol are off-road or have off-road sections.

Typical Cotswold countryside

LOCATION MAP

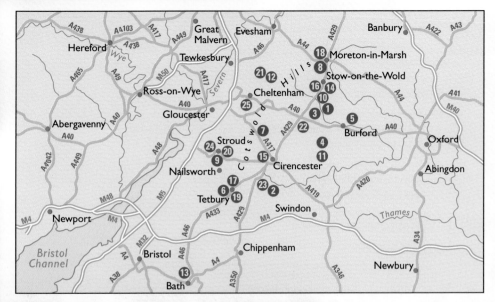

A438 A4103 A417 A449 Great Malvern Evesham A429 Banbury A422 A43

Hereford A438 M50 Wye Tewkesbury A46 A44 18 Moreton-in-Marsh

A465 A49 A417 Severn 21 12 8 Stow-on-the-Wold

Ross-on-Wye A40 Cheltenham 16 14 A44 A41

Gloucester 25 A40 10 A40 M40

Abergavenny A40 A48 7 A429 22 3 1 5 Burford A40 Oxford

A7042 A449 Stroud 24 20 4 Abingdon

Nailsworth 9 15 11 Cirencester A420

M48 M5 17 23 2 A419

M4 Newport M4 Tetbury 6 19 A433 A429 Swindon A34

Bristol Channel A4 Bristol A46 A4 Chippenham A346 Newbury

A38 13 A350 Bath Thames

KEY TO ROUTE MAPS

M23	Motorway		Cycle route	P	Parking
A259	'A' road / Dual carriageway		Optional route	☎	Telephone
B2130	'B' road / Dual carriageway	🚴	Start of cycle route	开	Picnic site
	Good minor road	12—	Route direction	▲	Camping site
	Minor road	B	Place of interest	👫	Public toilets
	Track / bridleway	🍺	Public house	☀	Viewpoint
	Railway / station	☕	Café / refreshments	†	Place of worship
	Canal / river	✕	Restaurant	▶	Golf course
	Lake	🛒	Convenience store	⁑	Tumulus
50	Contour (height in metres)		Height above sea level		
	Urban area				
	Woodland				

Height above sea level

| 50 | 100 | 150 | 200 | 300 metres |
| 165 | 330 | 490 | 655 | 980 feet |

INTRODUCTION

How to use this guide

Bartholomew's *Cycling in the Cotswolds* has been devised for all those who want trips out on their bicycles along quiet roads and tracks, passing interesting places and convenient refreshment stops without having to devise their own routes. Each of the 25 routes in this book has been compiled and ridden by an experienced cyclist for cyclists of all abilities.

Cycling in the Cotswolds is easy to use. Routes range from undemanding rides compiled specifically with families in mind to challenging full-day rides; the type of route is easily identified by colour coding (see page 5). At the start of each route an information box summarises: total distance (in kilometres/miles – distances have been rounded up or down throughout to the nearest 0.5km/mile and are approximate only); grade (easy, moderate or strenuous based on distance and difficulty); terrain; an average time to allow for the route; directions to the start of the route by car and, if appropriate, by train.

Each route is fully mapped and has concise, easy-to-follow directions. Comprehensive information on places of interest and convenient refreshment stops along each route are also given. Accumulated mileages within each route description give an indication of progress, while the profile diagram is a graphic representation of gradients along the route. These should be used as a guide only.

The following abbreviations are used in the route directions:

LHF	left hand fork
RHF	right hand fork
SO	straight on
SP	signpost
TJ	T junction
TL	turn left
TR	turn right
XR	crossroads

Cycling in the Cotswolds

The Cotswolds is one of Britain's most charming and popular tourist areas and those who cycle through the Cotswolds really get to know this beautiful part of the country; not only the popular places, but also the host of villages, lanes and rural beauty spots missed by those who visit by car or coach.

The word Cotswolds derives from *wolds*, meaning high open land, and *cod*, the old English man's name which was originally given to part of the north Cotswolds. The area known as the Cotswolds now extends much further, broadly stretching from Chipping Campden in the north, down the western scarp past Wotton-under-Edge, and to Fairford, Burford and Chipping Norton in the east.

The area is known for its hilly countryside, but there are gently undulating lanes with relatively few hills and although few routes in this book escape without hills in the ride, they are not all of the strenuous variety.

Geology, geography and history

The Cotswolds are mainly composed of Jurassic rocks deposited under the sea about 150 million years ago. The area was lifted on the western side by massive earth movements, creating the escarpment (ridge) which extends about 80.5km (50 miles) along the Cotswolds' western edge and rises 244-305m (800-1000 feet) from the clay vale, or valley, below. The hills up the face of the ridge are long and steep, but from the top of the ridge the land gently dips to the south east, forming the wolds – rolling countryside and gentle hills. Oolitic limestone is found over much of the Cotswolds and produces the honey coloured stone associated with the area. Between the layers of limestone is fuller's earth, a naturally absorbent clay which was used for cleaning (fulling) wool.

The Cotswolds were inhabited many thousands of years ago and the countryside is steeped in history. There are several Neolithic burial chambers and Hetty Pegler's Tump near Uley and Belas Knap south of Winchcombe are among the best preserved examples; the Rollright Stones are Bronze Age standing stones; and there are the remains of numerous Iron Age hill forts, such as Uley Bury.

The Romans conquered and developed the Cotswolds and there is still much evidence of their time here: in towns, e.g. Cirencester (*Corinium*) and Bath (*Aquae Sulis*); villas, such as that at Chedworth; and roads, many of which are still in use today – the Foss Way (from Bath through Cirencester to Stow-on-the-Wold and Moreton-in-Marsh), Akeman Street (running north east from Cirencester to Quenington), and Ryknild Street (from Lower Slaughter through Condicote to Weston).

Sudeley Castle (see Route 12)

The Saxons influenced the landscape by clearing trees and establishing farms. There are a number of village churches dating back to the Saxons, such as that at Daglingworth. The word *ley* derives from the Saxon word for a clearing, and is part of village names such as Alderley (alder clearing), Uley (Yew clearing) and Barnsley, Dursley and Coberley.

The prosperity of the Cotswolds continued after the Norman Conquest and much of the land was turned to pasture to support the growing numbers of sheep. During the Middle Ages the wool trade expanded: Cotswold wool and manufactured cloth was sold throughout the world. The geography of the area, with fast flowing streams, enabled the development of water powered mills, and fuller's earth, used in cleaning the cloth, was readily available. Chipping Campden, Cirencester, Fairford and Northleach were the homes of wealthy wool merchants, many of whom invested in the houses, mills and churches which are still a major feature of the Cotswolds today.

Much of the landscape seen today was created during the late 18th century, when thousands of acres of land was enclosed in order to create fields and increase agricultural production, and the miles of Cotswold dry stone walls were built.

Preparing for a cycling trip

Basic maintenance
A cycle ride is an immense pleasure, particularly on a warm sunny day. Nothing is better than coasting along a country lane gazing over the countryside. Unfortunately, not every cycling day is as perfect as this, and it is important to make sure that your bike is in good order and that you are taking the necessary clothing and supplies with you.

Before you go out on your bicycle check that everything is in order. Pump the tyres up if needed, and check that the brakes are working properly and that nothing is loose – the brakes are the only means of stopping quickly and safely. If there is a problem and you are not sure that you can fix it, take the bike to a cycle repair shop – they can often deal with small repairs very quickly.

When you go out cycling it is important to take either a puncture repair kit or a spare inner tube – it is often quicker to replace the inner tube in the event of a puncture, though it may be a good idea to practise first. You also need a pump, and with a slow puncture the pump may be enough to get you home. To remove the tyre you need a set of tyre levers. Other basic tools are an Allen key and a spanner. Some wheels on modern bikes can be removed by quick release levers built into the bike. Take a lock for your bike and if you have to leave it at any time, leave it in public view and locked through the frame and front wheel to something secure.

What to wear and take with you
It is not necessary to buy specialised cycling clothes. If it is not warm enough to wear shorts wear trousers which are easy to move in but fairly close to the leg below the knee – leggings are ideal – as this stops the trousers catching the chain. If you haven't got narrow-legged trousers, bicycle clips will hold them in. Jeans are not a good idea as they are rather tight and difficult to cycle in, and if they get wet they take a long time to dry. If your shorts or trousers are thin you might get a bit sore from being too long on the saddle. This problem can be reduced by using a gel saddle, and by wearing thicker, or extra, pants. Once you are a committed cyclist you can buy cycling shorts; or undershorts which have a protective pad built in and which can be worn under anything. It is a good idea to

wear several thin layers of clothes so that you can add or remove layers as necessary. A zip-fronted top gives easy temperature control. Make sure you have something warm and something waterproof.

If you wear shoes with a firm, flat sole you will be able to exert pressure on the pedals easily, and will have less work to do to make the bicycle move. Gloves not only keep your hands warm but protect them in the event that you come off, and cycling mittens which cushion your hands are not expensive. A helmet is not a legal requirement, but it will protect your head if you fall.

In general it is a good idea to wear bright clothing so that you can be easily seen by motorists, and this is particularly important when it is overcast or getting dark. If you might be out in the dark or twilight fit your bicycle with lights – by law your bicycle must have a reflector. You can also buy reflective bands for your ankles, or to wear over your shoulder and back, and these help motorists to see you.

You may be surprised how quickly you use up energy when cycling, and it is important to eat a carbohydrate meal before you set out. When planning a long ride, eat well the night before. You should eat small amounts of food regularly while you are cycling, or you may find that your energy suddenly disappears, particularly if there are hills or if the weather is cold. It is important to always carry something to eat with you – chocolate, bananas, biscuits – so that if you do start fading away you can restore yourself quickly. In warm weather you will sweat and use up fluid, and you always need to carry something to drink – water will do! Many bicycles have a fitment in which to put a water bottle, and if you don't have one a cycle shop should be able to fit one.

It is also a good idea to carry a small first aid kit. This should include elastoplasts or bandages, sunburn cream, and an anti-histamine in case you are stung by a passing insect.

It is a good idea to have a pannier to carry all these items. Some fit on the handlebars, some to the back of the seat and some onto a back rack. For a day's ride you probably won't need a lot of carrying capacity, but it is better to carry items in a pannier rather than in a rucksack on your back. Pack items that you are carrying carefully – loose items can be dangerous.

Getting to the start of the ride

If you are lucky you will be able to cycle to the start of the ride, but often transport is necessary. If you travel there by train, some sprinter services carry two bicycles without prior booking. Other services carry bicycles free in off-peak periods, but check the details with your local station. Alternatively, you could use your car – it may be possible to get a bike in the back of a hatchback if you take out the front wheel. There are inexpensive, easily fitted car racks which carry bicycles safely. Your local cycle store will be able to supply one to suit you.

Cycling on-road

Cycling on back roads is a delight with quiet lanes, interesting villages, good views and a smooth easy surface to coast along on. The cycle rides in this book are mainly on quiet roads but you sometimes cross busy roads or have stretches on B roads, and whatever sort of road you are on it is essential to ride safely. Always be aware of the possibility or existence of other traffic. Glance behind regularly, signal before you turn or change lane, and keep to the left. If there are motorists around, make sure that they have seen you before you cross their path. Cycling can be dangerous if you are competing for space with motor vehicles, many of which seem to have difficulty in seeing cyclists. When drivers are coming out of side

The village of Snowshill (see Routes 16 and 21)

roads, catch their eye before you ride in front of them.

You will find that many roads have potholes and uneven edges. They are much more difficult to spot when you are in a group because of the restricted view ahead, and therefore warnings need to be given. It is a good idea to cycle about a metre out into the road, conditions permitting, so that you avoid the worst of the uneven surfaces and to give you room to move in to the left if you are closely overtaken by a motor vehicle.

Other things to be careful of are slippery roads, particularly where there is mud or fallen leaves. Sudden rain after a period of dry weather often makes the roads extremely slippery. Dogs, too, are a hazard because they often move unpredictably, and sometimes like to chase cyclists. If you are not happy, stop or go slowly until the problem has passed.

Pedalling

Many modern bikes have 18 or 21 gears with three rings at the front and six or seven on the back wheel, and for much of the time you will find that the middle gear at the front with the range of gears at the back will be fine. Use your gears to find one that is easy to pedal along in so that your feet move round easily and you do not put too much pressure on your knees. If you are new to the bike and the gears it is a good idea to practise changing the gears on a stretch of flat, quiet road so that when you need to change gears quickly you will be ready to do so.

Cycling in a group

When cycling in a group it is essential to do so in a disciplined manner for your own, and others', safety. Do not ride too close to the bicycle in front of you – keep about a bicycle's length between you so that you will have space to brake or stop. Always keep both hands on the handlebars, except when signalling, etc. It is alright to cycle two abreast on quiet roads, but if it is necessary to change from cycling two abreast to single file this is usually done by the outside rider falling in behind the nearside rider; always cycle in single file where there are double white lines, on busy roads, or on narrow and winding roads where you have a restricted view of the road ahead. Overtake on the right (outside) only; do not overtake on the inside.

It is important to pass information to other members of the group, for example:

car up – a vehicle is coming up behind the group and will be overtaking;

car down – a vehicle is coming towards the group;

single up – get into single file;

stopping – stopping, or

slowing/easy – slowing due to junction, etc., ahead;

on the left – there is an obstacle on the left, e.g. pedestrian, parked car;

pothole – pothole (and point towards it).

Accidents
In case of an accident, stay calm and, if needed, ring the emergency services on 999. It is a good idea to carry a basic first aid kit and perhaps also one of the commercial foil wraps to put around anyone who has an accident to keep them warm. If someone comes off their bicycle move them and the bike off the road if it is safe to do so. Get someone in the party to warn approaching traffic to slow down, and if necessary ring for an ambulance.

Cycling off-road

All the routes in this book take you along legal rights of way – bridleways, byways open to all traffic and roads used as public paths – it is illegal to cycle along footpaths. Generally the off-road sections of the routes will be easy if the weather and ground are dry. If the weather has been wet and the ground is muddy, it is not a good idea to cycle along bridleways unless you do not mind getting dirty and unless you have a mountain bike which will not get blocked up with mud. In dry weather any bicycle will be able to cover the bridleway sections, but you may need to dismount if the path is very uneven.

Off-road cycling is different to cycling on the road. The average speed is lower, you will use more energy, your riding style will be different and there is a different set of rules to obey – the off-road code:

1 Give way to horse riders and pedestrians, and use a bell or call out to warn someone of your presence.

2 Take your rubbish with you.

3 Do not light fires.

4 Close gates behind you.

5 Do not interfere with wildlife, plants or trees.

6 Use only tracks where you have a right of way, or where the landowner has given you permission to ride.

7 Avoid back wheel skids, which can start erosion gulleys and ruin the bridleway.

Some of the off-road rides take you some miles from shelter and civilisation – take waterproofs, plenty of food and drink and basic tools – especially spare inner tubes and tyre repair equipment. Tell someone where you are going and approximately when you are due back. You are more likely to tumble off your bike riding off-road, so you should consider wearing a helmet and mittens with padded palms.

Local Tourist Information Centres

Burford
Sheep Street, Burford
Telephone (01993) 823558

Cheltenham
Municipal Offices, The Promenade, Cheltenham
Telephone (01242) 522878

Chipping Campden
Woolstaplers Hall Museum, High Street,
Chipping Campden
Telephone (01386) 840101

Cirencester
Corn Hall, Market Place, Cirencester
Telephone (01285) 654180

Nailsworth
1 Fountain Street, Nailsworth
Telephone (01453) 832532

Northleach
Cotswold Countryside Collection, Northleach
Telephone (01451) 860715

Painswick
The Library, Stroud Road, Painswick
Telephone (01452) 813552

Stow-on-the-Wold
Hollis House, The Square, Stow-on-the-Wold
Telephone (01451) 831082

Stroud
Subscription Rooms, Kendrick Street, Stroud
Telephone (01453) 765768

Tetbury
Old Courthouse, 63 Long Street, Tetbury
Telephone (01666) 503552

Winchcombe
The Town Hall, High Street, Winchcombe
Telephone (01242) 602925

Wotton-Under-Edge
The Heritage Centre, The Chipping,
Wotton-Under-Edge
Telephone (01453) 521451

Local cycle hire

Cotswold Cycling Company
48 Shurdington Road, Cheltenham
Telephone (01242) 250642

Country Lanes Cycle Centre
Station Forecourt, Moreton-in-Marsh
Telephone (01608) 650065

The Cycle Clinic
The Cross, Bath Road, Nailsworth
Telephone (01453) 835200

Pedal Power
8 Ashcroft Road, Cirencester
Telephone (01285) 640505

Local cycle shops

The Cycle Clinic and Pedal Power – see above.

Bike Tech
27 Pittville Street, Cheltenham
Telephone (01242) 251505

Crabtrees
50 Winchcombe Street, Cheltenham
Telephone (01242) 515291

Halfords
43 King Street, Stroud
Telephone (01453) 764571

Noah's Ark
London Road, Chalford, near Stroud
Telephone (01453) 884738

and 38 Clarence Street, Cheltenham
Telephone (01242) 251400

Severn Cycles
The Pikehouse, 23 Kingshill Road, Dursley
Telephone (01453) 544866

Severn Vale Cycles
223 Bath Road, Stroud
Telephone (01453) 755034

Thames and Cotswold Cycles
21 Church Street, Tetbury
Telephone (01666) 503490

Williams Cycles
82 Albion Street, Cheltenham
Telephone (01242) 512291

BOURTON-ON-THE-WATER AND THE SLAUGHTERS

Route information

Distance 15km (9.5 miles)

Grade Moderate

Terrain Undulating lanes and a stretch of bridleway. Children's bicycles will need gears for the few hills encountered on this route.

Time to allow 1-4 hours.

Getting there by car Bourton is just off the A429 between Stow-on-the-Wold and Northleach. There are several large car parks in the town.

Getting there by train There are no convenient rail links to the start of this route.

From Bourton to Lower Swell and the Slaughters. This undulating ride on quiet country lanes visits some of the most attractive and best known villages in the Cotswolds. The River Eye runs through the Slaughters and makes a focal point in both: Lower Slaughter is interesting to walk round; Upper Slaughter is a perfect spot for a picnic near the ford. The route also includes a short stretch of bridleway along the Roman Road Ryknild Street which continues to Condicote. The route crosses the A429 near Bourton, and particular care is needed there. This route is best undertaken outside the busiest tourist periods, as it is in a popular area for visitors.

Route description

From Bourton centre go north west along Lansdown to the A429.

1 TJ SP Stow TR – be careful crossing this busy road. Immediately TL SP Naunton.

2 SP Lower Slaughter TR.

3 TJ SP Upper Slaughter TL.

4 SP Upper Slaughter TR. As you go into the village bear left off the through road past the telephone box to the river and the ford. *3.5km (2 miles)*

5 Cross the ford and follow the road back to the through road and TL.

6 SP Cheltenham TL.

7 At B4068 SO onto bridleway signed Unsuitable for Motors. The bridleway was part of a Roman road.

8 XR no sign TR to Lower Swell. TR onto B4068. *9km (5.5 miles)*

9 Immediately after right turn, SP The Slaughters, TL.

10 At Lower Slaughter TR over bridge. It is worth exploring this lovely village. *12.5km (8 miles)*

11 TL no sign.

12 TJ SP Bourton-on-the-Water TL.

13 TJ SP Bourton-on-the-Water TL.

14 TR at A429 TJ SP Cirencester, then immediately TL along Lansdown, and back to Bourton-on-the-Water. *15km (9.5 miles)*

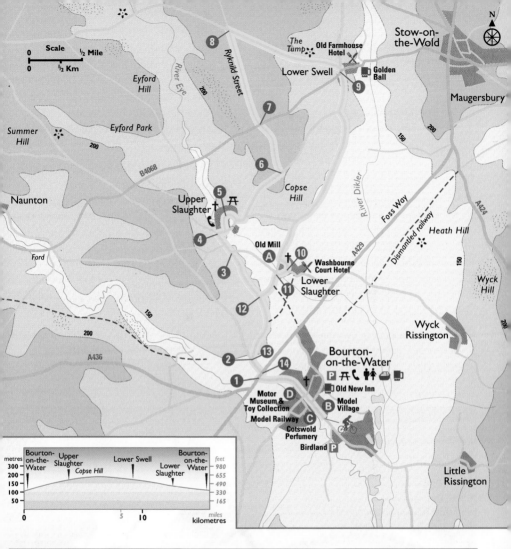

Food and drink

Bourton has numerous pubs, cafés and tearooms.

Washbourne Court Hotel, Lower Slaughter
Hotel close to the bridge in Lower Slaughter serving morning coffee, lunches and teas.

Golden Ball, Lower Swell
When you reach Lower Swell, TL onto B4068 and the pub is on the right. Real ale and bar snacks.

Old Farmhouse Hotel, Lower Swell
TL on the B4068 in Lower Swell – the hotel is on the left. Coffee, bar snacks and teas.

Places of interest along the route

Ⓐ Old Mill, Lower Slaughter
A mill museum with working water wheel and craft displays. Gift shop and antiques for sale, ice cream and refreshments. Open daily all year round 1000-1800. Charge. Telephone (01451) 820052.

Ⓑ Model Village, Bourton-on-the-Water
A model village, built in Cotswold stone, of Bourton as it was in 1937. The model village is situated behind the Old New Inn which has a bar, restaurant and garden. Open daily, in the summer 0900-1800 and in the winter 1000-1600. Charge. Telephone (01451) 820467

Ⓒ Cotswold Perfumery, Bourton-on-the-Water
A perfumery exhibition with audio-visual-scented show; a history of perfume; scented garden; a perfume quiz; and tips on how to choose a scent — it is the only exhibition of its kind in Europe. Gift shop. Open daily (except Christmas Day and Boxing Day) Monday to Saturday 0930-1700, Sunday 1030-1700. Charge for admission to exhibition. Telephone (01451) 820698.

Ⓓ Cotswold Motor Museum and Toy Collection, Bourton-on-the-Water
Beautiful cars and motorcycles and a magnificent collection of memorabilia, including a childhood toy collection and many period advertising signs. The museum is also home to Brum, the BBC children's programme character. Open daily from February to November 1000-1800. Charge. Telephone (01451) 821255.

Bourton Model Railway and Birdland are also of interest. See Route 10 for details.

Upper Slaughter

KEMBLE AND THE COTSWOLD WATER PARK

Route information

Distance 16.5km (10.5 miles)

Grade Easy

Terrain The ride is on quiet lanes and is virtually flat. There are one or two gentle slopes, but no hills.

Time to allow 1-3 hours.

Getting there by car Kemble is south west of Cirencester on the A429. You can park in the station car park (charge) or on the street in the village.

Getting there by train Kemble station is between Swindon and Stroud on the Paddington-Cheltenham line. For information telephone (0345) 484950.

From Kemble to Shorncote and on to Keynes and Neigh Bridge Country Parks. This is an easy ride in the flat countryside to the south of Cirencester. Keynes and Neigh Bridge Country Parks are part of the Cotswold Water Park, developed as a result of gravel extraction. There are over one hundred lakes, some of which are still being used for sand and gravel extraction. Most lakes are used for recreation including angling, sailing, windsurfing, canoeing and jet skiing. The River Thames starts at Thames Head about 1.5km (1 mile) north of Kemble, and you will cross it twice on this ride, between Kemble and Ewen, and again just before Neigh Bridge Country Park.

Places of interest along the route

Ⓐ Shorncote

This tiny rural hamlet was a medieval manor and, therefore, had its own church. The church has a late Norman chancel arch and the remains of 12th-century wall paintings. The church is now redundant and locked, but there is a note on the door telling you where to obtain the key.

Ⓑ Keynes Country Park

Country park with picnic sites, nature reserve, lakeside walks, barbecues (bring your own fuel) and a children's beach and paddling area. There is an information kiosk from which you can buy day tickets for angling and windsurfing. Car parking charge, but otherwise admission free. Always open, but restricted access for cars in winter. Telephone (01285) 861459.

Ⓒ Neigh Bridge Country Park

This country park has a picnic site, a play area and a lakeside walk. Day tickets for angling available at Keynes Country Park. Toilets (summer only). Always open and admission free. Telephone Keynes Country Park for information.

Route description

3 TR through Upper Siddington, over the bridge signed Weak Bridge and the old canal.

From Kemble, cycle eastwards SP Ewen. You will cross the head water of the River Thames.

1 TL SP Siddington.

2 TL SP Cirencester, then first right, SP Siddington. *6km (3.5 miles)*

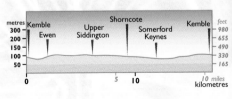

4 At TJ TR then first left (no signs).

5 At TJ TR then TL SP Shorncote.

6 At staggered XR TL. Keynes Country Park is on your left. ***10.5km (6.5 miles)***

7 TL out of Keynes Country Park.

8 TR SP Somerford Keynes, then SO SP Somerford Keynes.

9 TL SP Oaksey and over the River Thames again to Neigh Bridge Country Park on your right. ***12.5km (8 miles)***

10 XR TR onto Spine Road, then TR SP Old Mill Farm.

11 TR at TJ SP Kemble.

12 TL SP Kemble.

13 TL at TJ SP Tarlton and back into Kemble.
16.5km (10.5 miles)

Food and drink

Wild Duck Inn, Ewen
Keep SO for 90m (100 yards) in Ewen – the inn is on your right. Coffee and bar snacks available.

Bakers Arms, Somerford Keynes
TR as you enter Somerford Keynes – the pub is at the northern edge of the village. Coffee and bar snacks available.

Keynes Country Park

SHERBORNE BROOK AND THE RIVER WINDRUSH

Route information

Distance 18.5km (11.5 miles)

Grade Moderate

Terrain Along quiet lanes and through the undulating countryside south of Bourton-on-the-Water.

Time to allow 1-3 hours.

Getting there by car Sherborne is off the A40 south east of Cheltenham and close to the A429 north east of Cirencester. You can park by the side of the road in Sherborne.

Getting there by train There are no convenient rail links to the start of this route.

Places of interest along the route

A **Sherborne Park Estate, Sherborne**

The estate, owned by the National Trust, is a fine example of a traditional Cotswold estate. Access is by footpath only and there are extensive views over the Windrush Valley. The Estate adjoins Sherborne village, which was built as a model estate village in the mid-1800s. Always open with free admission. Telephone (01451) 844257 for further information.

B **Windrush Church, Windrush**

This delightful Norman church in the centre of the village has a fascinating south doorway with two rows of beakheads. Usually open, free admission.

Route description

From Sherborne to Great Rissington and the Barringtons. This ride, on quiet lanes, goes through traditional Cotswold countryside to the south of Bourton-on-the-Water. You will see stone walls, sheep in the fields and open farmland. The route is undulating, rather than hilly, starting at Sherborne Brook and descending twice to the River Windrush. There is a good picnic spot on the River Windrush, near Clapton-on-the-Hill.

From Sherborne go east through the village and, as the road turns sharp right, TL SP Clapton. Cycle up the hill and along an unfenced road to Clapton-on-the-Hill.

5km (3 miles)

1 Return for a short way back along road, away from Clapton-on-the-Hill.

2 TL at SP Unsuitable for Motors. This lane is narrow – the surface is uneven and there are usually pheasants wandering over it – so ride carefully. There is a lovely place to picnic down by the river.

3 TR at TJ (no sign) and go up through Great Rissington. **10km (6 miles)**

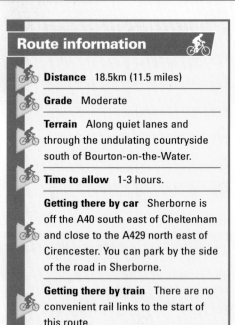

4 TR at TJ SP the Barringtons and freewheel down the hill to Great Barrington.

5 SO SP Little Barrington. You will pass the Fox Inn by the river. *14.5km (9 miles)*

6 TR SP Sherborne, along an undulating lane to Windrush and its church.

7 SO through Windrush and back to Sherborne. *18.5km (11.5 miles)*

Food and drink

The Lamb, Great Rissington
The pub is on the right as you go through the village. Real ales and bar snacks.

Fox Inn, Little Barrington
The pub is by the river as you leave Great Barrington. Morning coffee (from 1100), real ales and bar snacks.

BIBURY – ARLINGTON ROW AND THE TROUT FARM

Route information

Distance 19km (12 miles)

Grade Moderate

Terrain Quiet lanes through undulating countryside. The route is quite flat near Fairford, but there are a few small hills near Bibury.

Time to allow 1-3 hours.

Getting there by car Fairford is on the A417 between Cirencester and Lechlade. There is a free car park to the north of the church.

Getting there by train There are no convenient rail links to the start of this route.

The route starts in Fairford, an ancient market town, and takes in Bibury and the much photographed Arlington Row. William Morris described Bibury as the most beautiful village in England.

Places of interest along the route

A Fairford Church.
The perpendicular church is one of the great Cotswold wool churches and was built in the late 15th century by John Tame, a wealthy wool merchant. The church is famous for its medieval stained glass windows, the only complete set of such windows in the country. It also has lovely wood carvings and brasses. Open daily. Admission free.

B Arlington Row, Bibury
Arlington Row is a much photographed row of 17th-century weavers' cottages, looked after by the National Trust. You can walk up past them from the river. Always visible.

C Arlington Mill Museum, Bibury
There was a mill on this site as long ago as 1068. The present mill is 17th-century and contains a museum with exhibitions on the countryside and Victorian life. You can see the working mill machinery. Tea room and gift shop. Open daily from Easter to Christmas 1000-1800. Charge. Telephone (01285) 740368.

D Bibury Trout Farm
Landscaped water gardens, picnic areas, shop and refreshments. Open daily all year round (except Christmas and Boxing Day) Monday-Saturday, 0900-1700 (until 1800 in summer); Sunday 1000-1700. Charge. Telephone (01285) 740215.

Route description

TR out of car park along Mill Lane.

1 TR at TJ opposite Milton Farm.

2 TL SP Honeycomb Leaze.

4km (2.5 miles)

3 At Sunhill XR, SO SP Bibury.

4 TL at TJ SP Bibury. Then, TR SP Bibury at Ready Token – so called because coach drivers had to have their tolls ready.

5 TR XR SP Bibury and down to the centre of the 'most beautiful village in England' (William Morris). *9.5km (6 miles)*

6 SP Coln St. Aldwyns, TR with care at this blind corner.

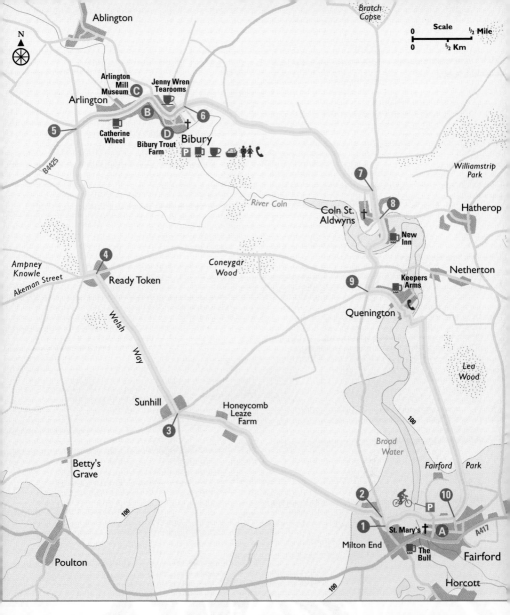

Ablington

Bratch
Copse

N

Scale
0 ——————— ½ Mile
0 ——————— ½ Km

Arlington
Mill
Museum **C**
Jenny Wren
Tearooms

Arlington

B

6

5

Catherine
Wheel

D

Bibury Trout
Farm

Bibury

🅿 ☕ ♿ 🚹 📞

B4425

Williamstrip
Park

River Coln

Coln St.
Aldwyns

7

8

Hatherop

New
Inn

Ampney
Knowle

Akeman Street

Ready Token

4

Coneygar
Wood

9

Keepers
Arms

Netherton

Quenington

Welsh
Way

Lea
Wood

Sunhill

3

Honeycomb
Leaze
Farm

Broad
Water

100

Betty's
Grave

Fairford   Park

2

10

🅿

100

St. Mary's †

A

1

A417

Poulton

Milton End

The
Bull

Fairford

100

Horcott

7　TR at TJ SP Coln St. Aldwyns and into the
village.　　　　　　　　　　**13.5km (8.5 miles)**

8　Arrive Coln St. Aldwyns XR. SO SP
Quenington.

9　At Quenington Green bear left down
through the village and over the River Coln.
Short hill ahead.

10　TR back into Fairford.　　**19km (12 miles)**

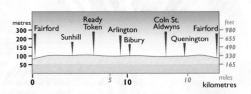

23

Food and drink

The Bull, Fairford
Situated in the Market Place, just south of the church. Coffee, real ales, bar snacks and teas.

Catherine Wheel, Bibury
On the right as you enter Bibury. Coffee (from 1100), real ales and bar snacks available.

Jenny Wren Tearooms, Bibury
Situated alongside the river, the tearooms offer morning coffee, lunches and teas.

New Inn, Coln St. Aldwyns
On the left as you go down through the village – bar snacks available.

Keepers Arms, Quenington
On your left, as you go down into the village; serving real ales and bar snacks.

Arlington Row, Bibury

BURFORD, SWINBROOK AND THE BARRINGTONS

Route information

Distance 23.5km (14.5 miles)

Grade Moderate

Terrain Quiet roads and some single track lanes through gently undulating countryside in the eastern Cotswolds.

Time to allow 2-3 hours.

Getting there by car Burford is on the A40 between Cheltenham and Oxford. There is a free car park near the church to the east of the High Street.

Getting there by train There are no convenient rail links to the start of this route.

This gentle ride, starting from Burford, goes along the River Windrush valley and crosses the river near the Barringtons and in Swinbrook. The ride is mostly on quiet roads, some of them single track with passing places. The eastern part of the ride is on the Oxfordshire Cycleway. Although there are a few gentle ups and downs, there are no steep hills. Little Barrington was home to a family of master masons, the Strongs, and also to a quarry located where the bowl-shaped village green is now. The Strongs worked under Sir Christopher Wren, when he was rebuilding parts of London after the Great Fire of 1666. Thomas Strong, who laid the foundation stone of St Paul's Cathedral, left money for the building of the bridge over the River Windrush in Little Barrington.

Places of interest along the route

A **Burford**

Cotswold town with a medieval bridge over the River Windrush. The long, wide High Street has a mix of grand houses, stone cottages and fascinating shops and gives the impression of having stood in its present garb for centuries. However, Burford, like many of the Cotswold small towns and villages, was rebuilt during the 15th century with the wealth from the expanding woollen industry. A survey of the buildings in Burford has revealed that the typical Cotswold honey-coloured stone is a façade added towards the end of the Middle Ages and behind it are the remains of the original timber-framed houses. In Burford is a 16th-century Tolsey or court house, with an open ground floor and half-timbered first floor. The Church of St John the Baptist has side chapels and fine monuments, particularly one to the Tanfield family. The churchyard contains a number of tombs which have tops in the shape of a bale of wool, reflecting the number of wealthy wool merchants who lived in the area. Admission to the church is free.

B **Swinbrook Church**

This lovely church will please both children and adults. Its most fascinating features are the Fettiplace family tombs near the altar – three Elizabethan and three Stuart Fettiplaces, each full size and each reclining on an elbow, looking around the church. The Redesdale family were local landowners, and two daughters, Nancy and Unity Mitford, are buried in the churchyard. Admission free.

Route description

Leave the car park, go over the bridge and TL. At XR TL.

1 TL, SP Swinbrook.

2 At XR SP Swinbrook, TL to Swinbrook.

4km (2.5 miles)

3 After passing through Swinbrook, go SO and continue along the Oxfordshire Cycleway.

4 TL at XR SP Burford.   *9.5km (6 miles)*

5 SO at XR SP Downs Lodge Farm, and along a single track road.

6 SP Taynton TR.

High Street, Burford

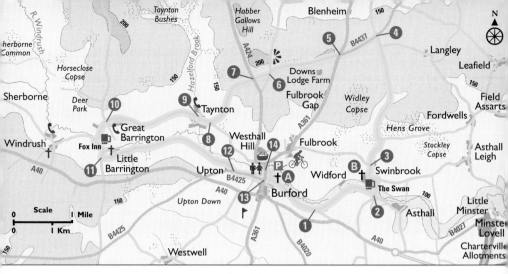

7 XR SP Taynton, SO.

8 TJ SP Taynton, TR into the village.
14km (8.5 miles)

9 SO to Great Barrington.

10 TL at TJ SP Little Barrington. You pass the Fox Inn by the river. _18km (11 miles)_

11 In Little Barrington TL (no SP). Pass the church and cycle along a quiet, undulating lane.

12 TJ (no SP) TL to Burford.

13 TJ TL into the centre of Burford.

14 TR along Church Lane back to the car park. _23.5km (14.5 miles)_

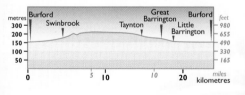

Food and drink

There are many pubs, cafés and tearooms in Burford.

The Swan, Swinbrook
Just over the river as you enter Swinbrook. Real ales and bar snacks available.

Fox Inn, Little Barrington
Beside the river, between Great Barrington and Little Barrington, serving coffee (from 1100), real ales and bar snacks.

Route 6
TETBURY, CHAVENAGE HOUSE AND CHERINGTON

Route information

Distance 24.5km (15 miles)

Grade Easy

Terrain Flat and gently undulating countryside to the north of Tetbury. The route follows quiet lanes.

Time to allow 2-4 hours.

Getting there by car Tetbury is on the B4014 south of Stroud, and on the A433 which runs south west from Cirencester. There are several car parks in Tetbury.

Getting there by train Kemble, about 14.5km (9 miles) from Tetbury, is the nearest station. For information telephone (0345) 484950.

This ride, mostly on unclassified roads, visits the relatively undiscovered Cotswolds between Stroud and Tetbury. The lanes run beside fields of crops, sheep and cattle and past the farms and hamlets that housed the agricultural workers. Tetbury was a wool town and has many attractive buildings. The elegant Gothic style parish church, St Mary's, was rebuilt in 1781. The large church windows contain pieces of medieval glass and the church itself still houses old box pews.

Tetbury's market place was laid out by AD 1200 – all Tetbury's old streets lead to it. The Market House, built in 1665 and used by the wool trade, rests on three rows of pillars. The Chipping, the site of a less important market, still has ancient remains of a Cistercian priory; the Chipping Steps are of medieval origin. Each spring Bank Holiday the Woolsack Races are held on Gumstool Hill in the town. Two teams race up and down the hill, between two pubs, carrying a 27kg (60 pound) sack of wool. The origins of the race go back over 400 years to when the drovers used to race each other in an effort to impress their young ladies.

Places of interest along the route

A Tetbury Police Museum, Tetbury
The museum is housed in the original cells of the old police station and contains many artefacts from the Gloucestershire Constabulary. Open from March to October, Monday-Saturday 1015-1615. Admission free. Telephone (01666) 503552 for further information.

B Chavenage House, Chavenage
Privately-owned Chavenage House is an Elizabethan manor house, constructed in 1576. The house contains fine 17th-century tapestries, furniture and relics of its Cromwellian associations. The house has been used many times as a location for television

28

productions. Each July the gardens provide the setting for a Shakespearean play and pre-performance picnics. Personal tours by the owner or members of his family are available. The house is open to the public on Easter Sunday and Easter Monday, and every Thursday and Sunday, from May to September 1400-1700. Charge. Telephone (01666) 502329 for further information.

Food and drink

Tetbury has a range of hotels, pubs and cafés. Recommended:

Two Toads Restaurant, Tetbury
Restaurant open daily, Monday-Saturday 0900-1630, Sunday 1000-1700.

Chavenage House

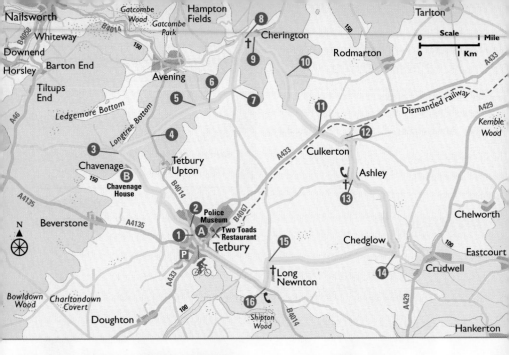

Route description

From the Market House in Tetbury, go along Long Street.

1 SO SP Avening.

2 At Five Trees Garden Centre, SP Chavenage, TL. You will pass Chavenage House on your left. **3.5km (2 miles)**

3 TR along a quiet lane (no SP).

4 Arrive B4014 and SO (no SP).

5 SO SP Cherington.

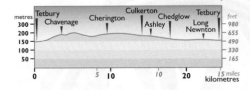

6 SO SP Cherington.

7 TL at TJ SP Cherington. The bench here is a good place to rest. **9.5km (6 miles)**

8 Follow the road through Cherington.

9 SO SP Rodmarton.

10 SO SP Culkerton.

11 At A433 SO, SP Culkerton.

12 TR SP Ashley. In the pond here, there is a duckhouse on stilts. **15.5km (9.5 miles)**

13 SO through Ashley.

14 TJ SP Long Newnton, TR. **21.5km (13.5 miles)**

15 TJ SP Long Newnton, TL.

16 At B4014 TR SP Tetbury to the end of the route. **24.5km (15 miles)**

THE DUNT VALLEY AND ITS CHURCHES

Route information

Distance 30km (18.5 miles)

Grade Moderate

Terrain Quiet country lanes in undulating countryside with some short, steep hills.

Time to allow 2-4 hours.

Getting there by car Elkstone is off the A417 south of Cheltenham. There is parking by the side of the road in Elkstone.

Getting there by train There are no convenient rail links to the start of this route.

From Elkstone, through the Duntisbournes and North Cerney, returning to Elkstone. This is a delightful ride on quiet, undulating lanes that take you both through and above the Dunt Valley. Some of the villages in the valley have fords – fun to cycle through, particularly on a summer's day. From any high point in the area, you will be able to see many spires and churches, and this ride passes four of the most beautiful churches in the Cotswolds. There are three pubs on the route but no shops, so take refreshments with you.

Places of interest along the route

A Elkstone Church
A lovely Norman church with many grotesque heads and a classic carved tympanum over the south door. The chancel has beautiful natural lighting. Usually open. Admission free.

B Duntisbourne Rouse Church
The church has Saxon remains – see the herring bone masonry in the north wall. The churchyard overlooks the Dunt stream and there is a scissor stile at the end of the path to the church. Usually open. Admission free.

C Daglingworth Church
This lovely church has four Saxon wall sculptures, so smooth they look modern. Note the tiny windows in the vestry wall. There are also interesting brass tablets in the floor of the porch. Usually open. Admission free.

D North Cerney Church
This fascinating church has Norman origins but was extensively restored and extended during the late 15th century. The stone altar dates from 1200. It was buried in the floor for nearly 400 years after the order, during the 16th century, that all stone altars must be destroyed, and was rediscovered in the 20th century. There are many carved heads both inside and outside the church and you can go up into the rood loft. Usually open. Admission free.

The Highwayman,
Beech Pike, near Elkstone
On the A417 between Elkstone and Winstone. Serves morning coffee (from 1100) and bar snacks.

The Bear, Perrott's Brook
The pub is on the right as you cross the A435. Morning coffee (from 1100), real ales and bar snacks available.

Bathhurst Arms, North Cerney
On the left of the A435 in the village, serving morning coffee, real ales and bar snacks.

Elkstone Church

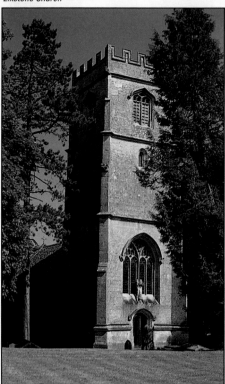

Route description

From Elkstone Church TL and ride south along an undulating road.

1   SO (with care) across the A417, SP Winstone.

2   TJ SP Sapperton TR.   *6km (3.5 miles)*

3   At Jackbarrow Farm TL, SP Duntisbourne Abbots 1 mile.

4   SO SP Birdlip, then TR down into Duntisbourne Abbots village.

5   TR at SP Ford. You can cycle through the ford or along the footpath.

6   At TJ (no sign) TL to Duntisbourne Leer ford – fun to ride through – and return back up the hill. You can see dovecotes in the cottage walls here.

7   TL SP Middle Duntisbourne.
   9.5km (6 miles)

8   TL down a steep hill to the ford, and then return back up the hill. TL SP Duntisbourne Rouse – you will pass the Saxon church on your left.

Note – a new trunk road is in the process of construction between Gloucester and Swindon. It will supersede parts of the A417 and A419. Route 7 will be affected in the following way: at direction 1 there will be an underbridge beneath the A417; between directions 11 and 12, just before the top of the hill from Daglingworth, take LHF to the Itlay Underpass under the A417, and at the far side TR onto Welsh Way and then TL to Perrott's Brook.

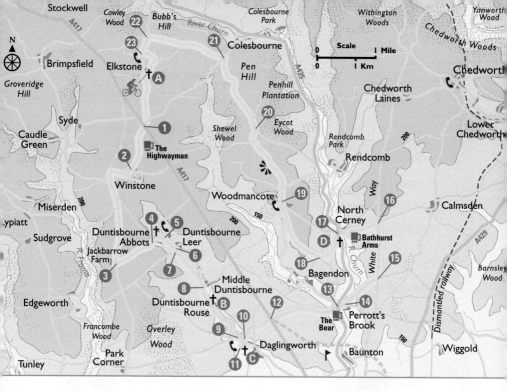

9   TJ TL into Daglingworth village.

10   XR TR SP church – short climb ahead.

11   Return to XR SP Perrott's Brook and SO, up another short steep hill.

12   Arrive A417 XR. SO SP Perrott's Brook.
14.5km (9 miles)

13   At A435 XR, SO SP Barnsley and cross Perrott's Brook.

14   TL (no SP).

15   XR TL SP Withington and cycle part way along the Roman road – the White Way.

16   TL SP North Cerney and into the village.
18.5km (11.5 miles)

17   At A435 TJ, TL. Then TR SP Bagendon. North Cerney Church is on your left, before another hill.

18   XR SP Woodmancote TR.

19   SO SP Colesbourne. There are good views down into the valley from along this road.

20   SO at TJ SP Elkstone.   *26km (16 miles)*

21   SO TJ SP Elkstone.

22   At XR SP Elkstone, TL.

23   At XR TL, SP Elkstone – the end of the ride and one of the highest Cotswold villages at 250m (820 feet).   *30km (18.5 miles)*

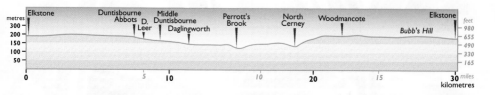

MORETON-IN-MARSH AND CHIPPING CAMPDEN LOOP

Route information

Distance 30.5km (19 miles)

Grade Moderate

Terrain Mostly unclassified roads, some narrow. Undulating farm land, but no major hills.

Time to allow 2-3 hours.

Getting there by car Moreton-in-Marsh is on the A429 (the Foss Way). Car parking is signposted. If no spaces are available, it is possible to park in the lane towards Batsford.

Getting there by train There is a railway station at the north end of Moreton's main street. This is on a secondary line between Worcester and Oxford. Telephone (0345) 484950 for information.

From Moreton-in-Marsh to Chipping Campden and back. Rolling countryside would adequately describe the landscape through which this route runs. From Moreton the route heads north east almost to Todenham before turning westwards towards Chipping Campden, one of the prettiest villages in the Cotswolds and very popular with tourists. The route then goes south to Blockley, a complicated little village with a maze of streets.

Places of interest along the route

Ⓐ Moreton-in-Marsh

Moreton-in-Marsh is an attractive north Cotswolds market town which stands on the line of the Roman Foss Way. The name Moreton-in-Marsh derives from 'farmstead on the moor'. The *marsh* is a corruption of *march*, meaning boundary. The long High Street is lined with interesting shops, houses and coaching inns. Of particular interest is the quaint stone tower with the bell turret. This structure is the curfew tower which was used to herald the curfew until as recently as 1860. The clock is 17th century. On the other side of the High Street is the neo-Tudor Market Hall, built in 1887. The parish church, to the east of the High Street, is Victorian.

Ⓑ Chipping Campden

Chipping Campden is a picturesque north Cotswolds town containing many old buildings; St James' Church, a landmark for miles around, open daily all year; the 17th-century Almshouses; Grevel's House, a fine example of 14th-century architecture; the Woolstaplers Hall, built in 1340; and the imposing Market Hall, built in 1627. The Old Silk Mill in Sheep Street was the home of the world renowned Guild of Handicrafts. The Guild moved to Chipping Campden from London in 1902 and although it closed in 1908, many of the craftsmen stayed and some of their descendents are still working in the Mill, where there is also an exhibition on the Guild of Handicrafts.

 Batsford Arboretum, Batsford

Designed and planted in the 1880s by Lord Redesdale on his return from a post in the British Embassy in Tokyo. There is a large variety of trees and shrubs and magnificent views over the Evenlode Vale. Also on the site is the Cotswold Falconry Centre (birds of prey are flown daily and you can see some of the more endangered species and their young), a garden centre, picnic area and teashop. The site can only be accessed from the A44 – from the route start point in Moreton-in-Marsh head south along the A429; at second roundabout with A44 TR taking care along this busy road. The site is a little way along on your right. The garden centre is open daily all year round 1000-1700; the Arboretum is open daily from March to October 1000-1700; and the Falconry Centre is open from March to October 1030-1700. Charge. Telephone (01608) 650722.

Food and drink

There are several pubs and cafés at the start and finish of the ride in Moreton, and in Chipping Campden, halfway round the ride. Refreshments are also available at Batsford Arboretum.

Ebrington Arms, Ebrington

Look carefully to your right as you enter Ebrington – the pub is on your right just before the first junction. Real ale and bar lunches available.

Bakers Arms, Broad Campden

The pub is on your left as you enter the village. Meals are available.

Old Coach House Tea Room, Blockley

Keep to the right of the church as you descend into Blockley and look to your left-hand side as the street bends – the tearoom is below the level of the roadway and not easy to see. Open at weekends and during school holidays 1200-1630, serving teas and coffees.

Crown Hotel, Blockley

Round the corner and along the street from the tearooms. Bar snacks available.

Clock tower on Market Hall, Moreton-in-Marsh

Route description

Start by the old tower in Moreton and head north in the direction of Stratford. Go over the railway bridge and almost immediately take RHF SP Todenham.

1 TL SP Stretton-on-Fosse and Paxford.

5km (3 miles)

2 At TJ with A429 TR, SP Stratford, and immediately TL SP Paxford.

3 TJ TL SP Paxford and Blockley.

10.5km (6.5 miles)

4 TR SP Ebrington.

5 TL at TJ (by Ebrington Arms) SP Mickleton and Chipping Campden and then immediately TL (no SP).

6 TL TJ SP Chipping Campden.

14.5km (9 miles)

7 After level crossing TR at TJ SP Chipping Campden.

Market Hall, Chipping Campden

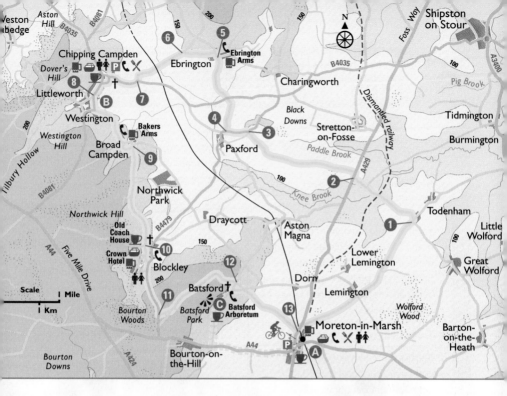

8 Negotiate Chipping Campden main street and TL SP Bourton, Moreton and Stow. At TJ SP Broad Campden and Blockley, TL.

9 TR SP Blockley and Moreton.
19.5km (12 miles)

10 In Blockley, keep SO to the right of the church. After right-hand bend TL and at TJ TR onto B4479.

11 TL SP Batsford and Aston Magna.
24.5km (15 miles)

12 TR to Batsford village. Then TL and at XR TR.

13 TJ SP Cirencester, TR and return to starting point. *30.5km (19 miles)*

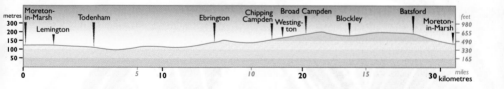

PAINSWICK AND THE NORTHERN STROUDWATER VALLEYS

Route information

Distance 32.5km (20 miles)

Grade Strenuous

Terrain Apart from brief stints along A and B roads, the circuit is along quiet unclassified lanes, a number of them narrow. Hills are numerous and some are steep. Low gears would be a decided asset.

Time to allow 3-4 hours

Getting there by car Stroud is 8km (5 miles) east of the M5. It is approached from the east by the A419 and from the north and south by the A46.

Getting there by train There is a railway station in Stroud, on the line between Gloucester and Swindon. Telephone (0345) 484950 for information.

From Stroud to Painswick and back. Stroud itself is at the focus of five valleys, making the landscape different to the rolling wolds further north and east. The route starts up the Slad valley, through Cider with Rosie country – the author Laurie Lee was brought up in the village of Slad and still lives there. From the Slad Valley the route goes into the Painswick valley and then descends the steep flank of the Main valley. It is a scenic ride with plenty of views to enjoy. Trees are an integral part of the landscape here and the route is seldom far from woodland.

Places of interest along the route

A Prinknash Abbey and Pottery, Cranham
Prinknash Abbey and Pottery are based in a modern Abbey, completed for the Benedictine monastic community in 1972. A tour of the pottery can be made, lasting approximately 20 minutes. There is a pottery gift shop, tearoom, and picnic and children's play area. The Abbey church, set in attractive grounds, can be visited and is open daily 0500-2100, admission free. Pottery tours are available Monday-Saturday 1030-1600 and Sunday afternoons (closed for lunch 1230-1330). Charge. The gift shop is open daily 0900-1730 and the tearoom open 0930-1700. Telephone (0345) 812239.

B Prinknash Bird Park, Prinknash Abbey, Cranham
Created in 1974, the Prinknash Bird Park is situated in the grounds of Prinknash Abbey. The park comprises woodland, footpaths, ponds and lakes and contains peacocks, many varieties of geese, swans, ducks, pheasants and other birds. The ponds are teeming with fish, which you can feed, and there are African pygmy goats and a herd of fallow deer. There is also an aviary containing noisy, colourful and

exotic birds. Gift shop, tearoom and picnic area. Open daily throughout the year 1000-1700. Charge. Telephone (01452) 812727.

ⒸPainswick Antiques and Craft Centre, Painswick

The Antiques and Craft Centre is housed in a converted Georgian chapel. On the first floor are local crafts, including knitware, wood craft and pictures, and on the ground floor are antiques and collectables to suit all tastes and pockets. Open daily all year round, Monday-Friday 1000-1700, Saturday 0930-1730, Sunday 1100-1730. Admission free. Telephone (01452) 812431.

ⒹPainswick Rococo Garden, Painswick House, Painswick

The Rococo period in garden design occurred between the formal styles of the 17th century and the more natural styling of the 18th century. The Rococo garden at Painswick, covering 2.5 hectares (6 acres), is the country's only complete survivor of this style and is being restored to its original form. There are formal vistas as well as woodland walks. Gift shop and restaurant (open Wednesday-Sunday). The garden is open from the second Wednesday in January to the end of November, Wednesday-Sunday, on Bank Holidays and daily during July and August, 1100-1700. Charge. Telephone (01452) 813204.

ⒺHaresfield Beacon, Stonehouse

Haresfield Beacon, comprising ancient ramparts and earthworks, is a National Trust site set 213m (700 feet) above sea level on a hilltop at the edge of the Cotswold ridge. Great views over Standish Wood, the Malvern Hills, Severn Vale and the Welsh mountains.

Standish Wood viewed from Haresfield Beacon

Route description

The route starts from the Greyhound Inn at the XR of High Street, King Street, Gloucester Street and Lansdown. Cycle along Lansdown and after 0.5km (0.3 mile) TR at XR and head up the B4070.

1 LHF at Bulls Cross SP Sheepscombe (views towards Painswick on left).

5km (3 miles)

2 TL SP Sheepscombe village (opposite Methodist Chapel).

3 TR SP Cranham.

4 TR SP Cranham.

5 After passing Cranham Church (note the shears sculpted high on the church tower – a symbol of the sheep trade) emerge onto Cranham Common and take the LHF to village.

11km (7 miles)

6 TL at TJ by village hall. No SP.

7 At TJ TL along Buckholt Road. Almost immediately, TL along A46 or TR to Prinknash Abbey.

8 Take second left off A46, SP Sheepscombe. Steep descent then a climb to eventually retrace about 300 metres of outward journey. TR (no SP but footpath sign pointing left).

9 TJ TR at Painswick Lodge Gate TJ. No SP.

15.5km (9.5 miles)

10 Arrive TJ with A46 and TL.

11 Arrive Painswick – past the traffic lights to see the village. Look for the churchyard with altar tombs and (reputedly) 99 yew trees; a set of 17th-century stocks outside the wall at the back of the churchyard; Painswick Antiques and Craft Centre. To continue the route, return to XR (traffic light controlled) and TL onto B4073, SP Gloucester. About 700 metres along this road is the entrance to Painswick House and the Rococo Garden. A further 1.5km (1 mile) brings you opposite the summit of Painswick Beacon – it is a comparatively short walk to the trig point and long-distance views.

Food and drink

Stroud has a number of cafés and pubs and there is a café at Tescos in Stroud, which you pass towards the end of the route. Refreshments are also available at Prinknash Abbey, Prinknash Bird Park and Painswick Rococo Garden.

Woolpack Inn, Slad
A popular pub and a centre of village social life. Bar snacks available.

Butchers Arms, Sheepscombe
A 17th-century pub – traditional ales, bar snacks and restaurant.

Falcon Inn, Painswick
Bar meals, tearoom and gardens.

St Michaels Restaurant, Painswick
Morning coffee, lunches and cream teas. Closed Mondays except Bank Holidays.

Chancellors, Painswick
Tearoom and licensed restaurant. Open every day during the summer (closed Wednesdays at other times of the year).

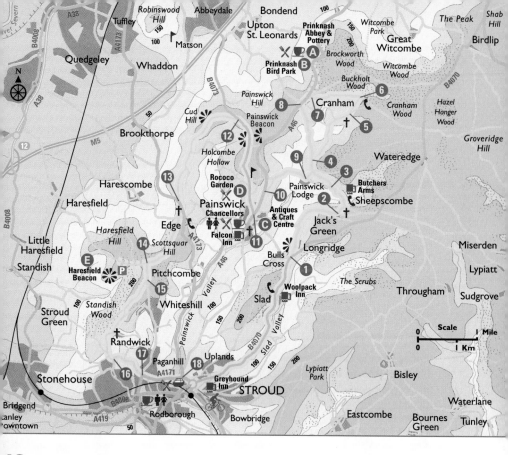

12 TL SP Edge. Fine views of Gloucester and the Malvern Hills.

13 TJ TL onto A4173, SP Edge. Almost immediately, RHF SP Whiteshill and Randwick.
24.5km (15 miles)

14 SO to Haresfield Beacon or, to continue route, follow road round to the left.

15 TR SP Randwick.

16 Arrive junction at Townsend. SO, SP Ruscombe and Whiteshill.

17 After passing the Old Crown Inn TJ (note remnant of Maypole), TR then immediately left at mini roundabout at A4171.

18 TJ (mini roundabout), TR SP Cirencester and Bath. SO at next mini roundabout and climb Gloucester Street back to the finish point at the Greyhound Inn. *32.5km (20.5 miles)*

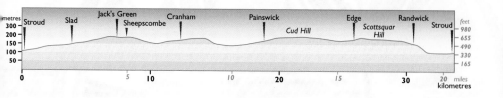

BOURTON, THE BARRINGTONS AND THE RISSINGTONS

Route information

Distance 33.5kms (21 miles)

Grade Moderate

Terrain Apart from a short stretch on the A429, the route is on unclassified roads – a long and steep climb, undulating lanes and a charming run along the valley of the Sherborne Brook.

Time to allow 2-3 hours.

Getting there by car Bourton-on-the-Water is to the east of the A429 (the Foss Way). Car parking is signposted.

Getting there by train Kingham, to the east of Bourton, is the nearest station – about 8km (5 miles) from the nearest point of the route (direction 9). Kingham station is on a secondary line between Worcester and Oxford. Telephone (0345) 484950 for information.

From Bourton-on-the-Water through Farmington and the Barrington and Rissington villages. The ride starts with a steep hill out of Bourton – when you see a road coming in from the right, you have almost reached the top of the hill. The route then goes eastwards to the villages of Little and Great Barrington, before heading north to the Rissingtons – Great, Little and Wyck Rissington.

Places of interest along the route

A **Bourton-on-the-Water**

This old world Cotswold village, the site of a settlement since pre-Roman times, is always thronged with visitors. There is plenty to see and do. The **Model Village** is a replica of Bourton itself, built of local stone at one-ninth scale. Open daily, in the summer 0900-1600 and in the winter 1000-1600. Charge. Telephone (01451) 820467. **Birdland** has tropical birds and the less tropical penguins. Picnic area, children's play area, gardens and cafeteria. Open from March to October 1000-1800; from November to February 1000-1600. Charge. Telephone (01451) 820480. **Bourton Model Railway** is one of the finest indoor model railway layouts in the country. Over 40 British and Continental trains run automatically through imaginative scenery. There is a model and toy shop. Open daily from April to September 1100-1730; from October to March at weekends only 1100-1700. Charge. Telephone (01451) 820686. The **Cotswold Motor Museum and Toy Collection** has cars, motorcycles, pedal-powered vehicles, caravans, a magnificent collection of memorabilia, period advertising signs and a childhood toy collection. Open daily from February to November 1000-1800. Charge. Telephone (01451) 821255. The **Cotswold Perfumery** is a unique experience and the only exhibition of its kind in Europe – an audio 'smelly-vision' display, an ingredients room, perfume quiz and perfumed garden. Gift shop. Open daily (except Christmas Day and Boxing Day) Monday to

Saturday 0930-1700, Sunday 1030-1700. Charge for admission to exhibition. Telephone (01451) 820698.

B **Sherborne Park Estate, Sherborne**

Owned by the National Trust, this is a fine example of a traditional Cotswold estate. Access is by footpath only and there are extensive views over the Windrush Valley. The Estate adjoins Sherborne village, which was built as a model estate village in the mid-1800s. The Estate is always open, with free admission. Telephone (01451) 844257 for further information.

Food and drink

There are numerous opportunities for refreshment in Bourton-on-the-Water.

Fox Inn, Little Barrington
Situated between Little Barrington and Great Barrington, at direction 5, with a terrace overlooking the River Windrush. Meals are available all day.

The Lamb, Great Rissington
In front of you as you descend the hill into the village. Meals available.

Coach and Horses Inn, Bourton
On the A429 as you enter Bourton. Bar meals available.

The Model Village, Bourton-on-the Water

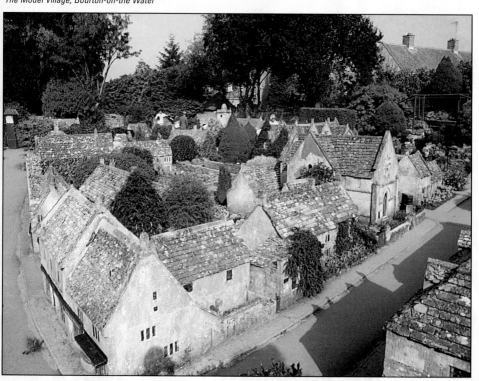

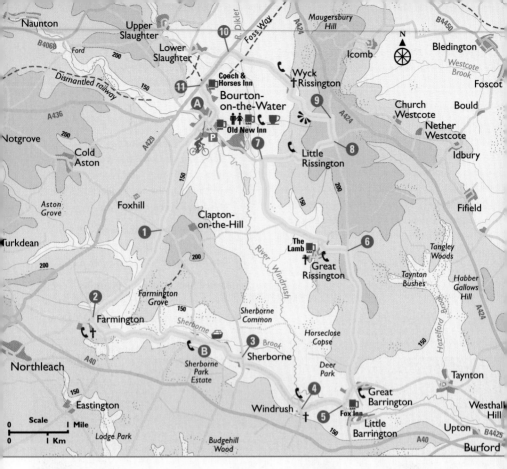

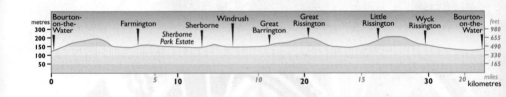

Route description

From the centre of Bourton-on-the-Water, cross the river bridge opposite the Edinburgh Woollen Mill and cycle along Sherborne Street in a south westerly direction.

1 TR SP Farmington. *5km (3 miles)*

2 Arrive Farmington. Take LHF then TL. The structure on the green to the right is a pump house presented by citizens of Farmington, Connecticut, USA. *8.5km (5 miles)*

3 Arrive Sherborne and TR at TJ, then TL SP Windrush and the Barringtons.

4 XR TL (to left of church) SP the Barringtons. *15.5km (9.5 miles)*

5 TL to cross River Windrush, SP Great Barrington and the Rissingtons. Keep left in Great Barrington.

6 TL SP Great Rissington and Bourton. *21.5km (13.5 miles)*

7 TJ TR, SP Little Rissington and Burford. *25.5km (16 miles)*

8 TL at XR, SP Stow-on-the-Wold.

9 TL SP Wyck Rissington. *28.5 km (17.5 miles)*

10 Arrive at A429 (the Foss Way). TL SP Cirencester and Cheltenham.

11 TL SP Bourton, to the finish of the route. *33.5km (21 miles)*

Terraced cottages on Sherborne Park Estate

Route information

Distance 36.5km (23 miles)

Grade Moderate

Terrain Quiet lanes in gently undulating countryside. There are one or two short hills and a few downhill slopes.

Time to allow 2-4 hours.

Getting there by car Fairford is on the A417 between Cirencester and Lechlade. There is a free long stay car park north of Fairford Church.

Getting there by train There are no convenient rail links to the start of this route.

This lovely ride in the eastern Cotswolds visits several picture postcard villages. A figure of eight route takes you from Fairford to Eastleach Turville and Eastleach Martin, on either side of the River Leach; on to Filkins and Shilton on Shill Brook, where there is a delightful picnic spot; and back over the River Leach to Fairford. Despite being in Oxfordshire, Filkins has a typical Cotswolds' character: its buildings are constructed from locally quarried stone; and huge rectangular slabs of stone, actually stone tiles, edge many of the cottage gardens. Fairford's prosperity in the late Middle Ages was almost exclusively due to the Tames, one of the Cotswolds' wealthiest wool merchant families, who were responsible for building

Fairford Church. Fairford was an important staging post between London and Gloucester and the 17th- and 18th-century buildings in the High Street and Market Place reflect this.

Places of interest along the route

Ⓐ Fairford Church, Fairford
This is one of the great Cotswold wool churches. It was built in the late 15th century and was paid for by the Tame family, wealthy wool merchants. It has restored medieval stained glass windows – the only complete set of such windows in the country. There are also brasses and wood carvings. Open daily, all year round. Admission free.

Ⓑ Eastleach Martin and Eastleach Turville.
The villages are on opposite sides of the River Leach and you can walk from one to the other over an attractive old stone footbridge. Each village has its own church; the Turville church has a saddleback tower and a Norman doorway; the Martin church – now redundant – has medieval benches and some of the best examples of decorated windows in the Cotswolds. Open daily all year round. Admission free.

Ⓒ Cotswold Woollen Weavers, Filkins, near Lechlade
Manufacturers and retailers of fine woollens. At this traditional Cotswold woollen mill you can see the weaving taking place and visit the well stocked mill shop. There is an exhibition on the history of wool in the Cotswolds, coffee shop and picnic area. Open daily all year round

(except 25-31 December), Monday to Saturday 1000-1800; Sunday 1400-1800. Free admission. Telephone (01367) 860491.

**Ⓓ Cotswold Wildlife Park,
Bradwell Grove, Burford**

Set in 48.5 hectares (120 acres) of parkland, the Wildlife Park was first opened in 1970 and has a vast collection of animals from all over the world. There are rhinos, zebras and ostriches, tigers and leopards, monkeys, otters and tropical birds, as well as a reptile house, aquarium, insect house and fruit bat exhibition. You can watch the penguins being fed at 1100 and 1600 everyday (except Fridays). Children's playground, narrow gauge railway, picnic areas and cafeteria. Open daily all year round (except Christmas Day) 1000-1800, or dusk if earlier. Charge. Telephone (01993) 823006.

Food and drink

Refreshments are available at the Cotswold Woollen Weavers and the Cotswold Wildlife Park.

Ⓘ The Bull, Fairford
Situated in the Market Place, south of Fairford Church. Morning coffee, real ales, bar snacks and teas available.

Ⓘ Victoria Inn, Eastleach
The pub is on raised ground to the left as you enter the village. Real ales and bar snacks available.

Ⓘ Five Alls, Filkins
TR at TJ as you enter the village. The pub serves real ales and bar snacks.

Ⓘ Rose and Crown, Shilton
Continue past the pond in Shilton and the pub is on the left. Real ales and bar snacks.

Ⓘ The Swan, Southrop
In the village centre, serving real ales and bar snacks.

Typical stone cottages, Filkins

Route description

TL out of car park behind Fairford Church and go along Park Street. TR SP Lechlade, and first left (unsigned) along Hatherop Road to the edge of the town.

1 TL at TJ (no SP).

2 TR SP Eastleach. **4km (2.5 miles)**

3 SO at XR SP Eastleach. Continue along a gently undulating road.

4 TR SP Eastleach. In the village, look out for the old stone footbridge over the river.
8km (5 miles)

5 Bear right, SP Filkins, and along a flat, quiet road into Oxfordshire.

6 TR TJ SP Lechlade. Then TR SP Filkins and go under the A361.

7 TJ in Filkins, TL. Cotswold Woollen Weavers are on the left. To continue the route, TL out of the mill. **12.5km (8 miles)**

8 TR SP Broadwell.

9 TL XR (no SP) and SO at next XR. Brize Norton Airfield is nearby, so you may see low-flying transport planes overhead.

10 TL SP Carterton.

11 TL SP Shilton.

12 TR at TJ SP Shilton and cycle down the hill into the village. **19.5km (12 miles)**

13 Return back up the hill and SO SP Holwell.

Eastleach Martin Church viewed from Eastleach Turville

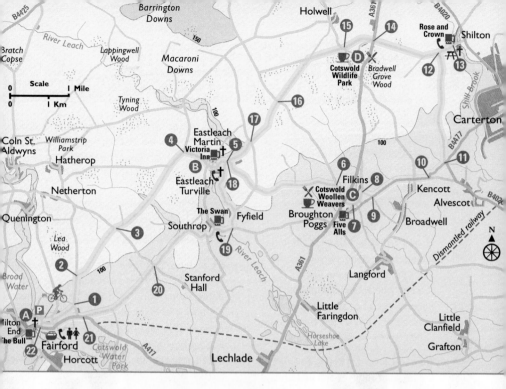

14 Arrive A361 XR. SO SP Holwell. The Cotswold Wildlife Park is on the left.

23km (14.5 miles)

15 SO at XR, SP Eastleach Martin, and through open, undulating countryside.

16 SO at XR SP Eastleach Martin.

17 SO at XR SP Eastleach, and back into Eastleaches. *28km (17.5 miles)*

18 SO at XR SP Southrop, riding parallel to the River Leach.

19 TR TJ SP Southrop and into the village. Continue out of the village and keep left at XR.

30.5km (19 miles)

20 At XR SO, SP Fairford, and across farmland.

21 Arrive TJ A417. TR SP Cirencester (with care) and along to Fairford Market Place.

22 TR into Fairford Market Place and return to the car park. *36.5km (22.5 miles)*

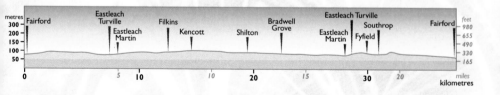

SUDELEY CASTLE, GUITING POWER AND STANWAY HOUSE

Route information

Distance   37km (23 miles)

Grade   Moderate

Terrain   Unclassified roads, some narrow, and B roads. There is a long, steep climb early in the ride and after this the route passes through typical undulating Wold country. There are two alternative off-road sections on this route, which merit a strenuous grading.

Time to allow   2-4 hours. Following the off-road sections will add around one hour to the riding time.

Getting there by car   Winchcombe can be reached from Cheltenham in the south or Stratford in the north, on the B4632. There are signposted car parks in the town.

Getting there by train   Cheltenham is the nearest station, 16km (10 miles) from Winchcombe, and is on the main line between Birmingham and Bristol. Telephone (0345) 484950 for information.

From Winchcombe to the upper levels of the Cotswolds. Only those who are very fit and equipped with the lowest of gears will not walk this hill, but the scenery compensates for all the hard work. At Brockhampton the route turns eastwards over the Wolds to Salperton,

then heads north to Guiting Power. Stumps Cross marks the start of a longish descent towards Stanway and Toddington. The return to Winchcombe is along the B4632.

Places of interest along the route

A **Sudeley Castle and Gardens, Winchcombe**
The castle, once the palace of Katherine Parr, dates from 1440. There are beautiful formal gardens, a wildfowl sanctuary, a shop and plant centre, adventure playground, tearooms and licensed restaurant. Open daily from March to October 1030-1730. Charge. Telephone (01242) 603197.

B **Belas Knap, south of Winchcombe**
Belas Knap is one of the best preserved and restored long barrows in the Cotswolds. It stands on a hilltop more than 290m (950 feet) high above sea level and was probably constructed around 3000BC. As a tomb, Belas Knap would have been used for a number of successive years until the burial chambers were deliberately blocked. The name Belas Knap is probably derived from old English: *bel* a beacon; *cnaepp* a hilltop. The site is maintained by English Heritage and there is no admission charge. Telephone (01179) 750700 for further information.

C **Cotswold Farm Park, Guiting Power**
The premier rare breed survival centre in the country. The Cotswold Farm Park is home to rare breeds of British sheep, cattle, pigs, goats, horses, poultry and waterfowl. Lots of newborn animals to see throughout the year, as well as

special weekend events such as working dog demonstrations, a vintage tractor rally and a goat weekend. Nature farm trail, pets' corner, children's shop and playground, café. Open daily from April to October 1030-1700, and until 1800 on Sundays, Bank Holidays and throughout July and August. Charge. Telephone (01451) 850307.

Ⓓ Stanway House, Stanway

A most romantic Jacobean manor house, with plenty to see: family portraits, gatehouse, old brewery, Medieval tithe barn, extensive grounds and formal gardens. Open from June to September, Tuesday-Thursday, 1400-1700. Charge. Telephone (01386) 584469.

Ⓔ Gloucestershire & Warwickshire Steam Railway, Toddington

Steam and diesel locomotives run from the restored station at Toddington, to the rebuilt station at Winchcombe and through a tunnel to Gretton and beyond, before returning to Toddington. Special events such as Friends of Thomas [the Tank Engine] and Steam Galas are held at weekends throughout the year. Picnic area, shop and tearoom at Toddington. The railway is open all year round with variable services, first daily departure around mid-morning, the last in the early evening. Admission to Toddington Station is free but there is a charge for train journeys. Telephone (01242) 621405 for a talking timetable.

Food and drink

There are several pubs and cafés in Winchcombe and refreshments are available at Sudeley Castle, the Cotswold Farm Park and Toddington Station.

Ⓒ Craven Arms, Brockhampton

Cross the infant river Coln and climb through the village – the Craven Arms is down a side turning to the right. Meals available.

Ⓒ Farmers Arms, Guiting Power

On your left-hand side as you TR into the village. A popular pub serving morning coffee, meals, real ale and hot and cold snacks.

Ⓒ Halfway House, Kineton

On your right as you go through the village. Coffee, meals, and hot and cold snacks available.

Ⓒ Old Bakehouse, Stanway

Open for afternoon tea daily from Easter (except Mondays and Wednesdays) 1500-1800.

Ⓒ Pheasant Inn, Toddington

On the roundabout at the intersection of the B4632 and the B4077. Home cooked food and real ale.

Route description

From Winchcombe Church head south west, towards Cheltenham, on the B4632.

1 LHF SP Brockhampton and Andoversford and immediately TL into Corndean Lane.
As you start to climb the hill look left for view of Sudeley Castle.

2 To follow the off-road section:

a SO, SP Corndean Lane.

b Keep left SP Hill Barn Farm and continue uphill.

c TL past old stables at Wontley Farm and go downhill and through the gates.

d Go through gate and on between house and barn. The track then becomes road.

e At XR, TR SP Brockhampton and Andoversford to continue route at direction 4.

Otherwise, TL SP Charlton Abbots and Andoversford. Shortly afterwards look for a footpath on right to Belas Knap, an 800m (0.5 mile) walk.

3 XR SO, SP Brockhampton and Andoversford. *6km (3.5 miles)*

4 XR TL, SP Brockhampton and Stow-on-the-Wold.

5 Arrive XR with A436 and SO (no SP). *10.5km (6.5 miles)*

6 TL, SP Salperton.

7 Cross the A436 again at TJ and TR onto B4068. *14.5km (9miles)*

8 Arrive multiple junction and TL (sharply, between pillars).

9 TJ TR (no SP).

10 Arrive Guiting Power at TJ. TL then immediately TR to go past the Farmers Arms pub. *19.5km (12 miles)*

11 TL at TJ and to continue the on-road route go to direction 12. To follow the off-road section:

a At staggered XR, TL SP Roel Gate and Charlton Abbots.

b Cycle through the ford and up to a junction with a track and a road. TR opposite car park SP and cycle on to the house. Keep right through gate and continue through wood and past a lake.

c TL at TJ.

d TR SP Ford and Cutsdean – note the views to Evesham Vale.

e TL SP Farmcote then almost immediately TR up bridleway and through gate.

f Footpath goes left, but continue SO.

g Arrive B4077 and TL down Stanway Hill to continue the route at direction 13.

12 At XR TL onto B4077, SP Tewkesbury, and go down Stanway Hill. *26km (16 miles)*

13 At XR (roundabout) TL SP Winchcombe (31.5km/19.5 miles) and return to Winchcombe on the B4632. *37km (23 miles)*

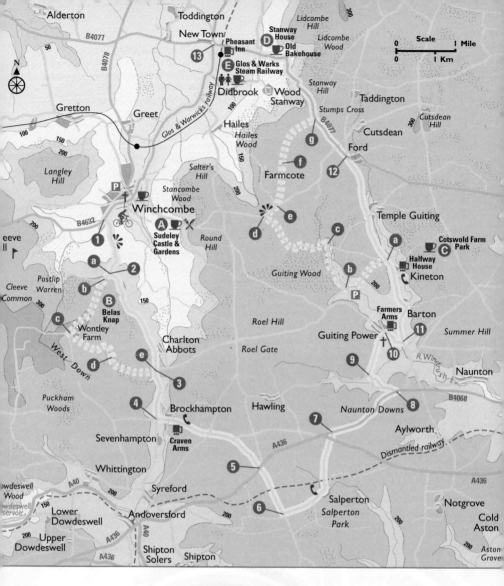

Alderton

Toddington

New Town

B4077

B4078

Lidcombe Hill

300

Stanway House

D Old Bakehouse

E Glos & Warks Steam Railway

13

Pheasant Inn

Lidcombe Wood

Stanway Hill

Taddington

N

50

Gretton

Greet

Glos & Warwicks railway

Didbrook

Wood Stanway

Stumps Cross

B4077

Cutsdean

Cutsdean Hill

300

Hailes

Hailes Wood

100

150

Ford

12

Scale

0   1 Mile
0   1 Km

100

150

200

Langley Hill

Salter's Hill

Stancombe Wood

200

g

f

Farmcote

Temple Guiting

P

B4632

Winchcombe

A Sudeley Castle & Gardens

Round Hill

e

d

c

a

C Cotswold Farm Park

Halfway House

Kineton

eeve II

200

1

a

2

b

150

Guiting Wood

b

P

200

Postlip Warren

Cleeve Common

300

B Belas Knap

c

Wontley Farm

Roel Hill

Farmers Arms

Barton

Summer Hill

West Down

d

e

3

Charlton Abbots

Roel Gate

Guiting Power

10

11

R. Windrush

Naunton

Puckham Woods

4

Brockhampton

Craven Arms

Hawling

Naunton Downs

9

8

B4068

Aylworth

Sevenhampton

7

Whittington

5

A436

Dismantled railway

A436

owdeswell Wood

A40

200

Syreford

6

Salperton

Salperton Park

Notgrove

Cold Aston

wdeswell servoir

150

Lower Dowdeswell

Andoversford

A40

200

Upper Dowdeswell

200

A436

A436

Shipton Solers

Shipton

Aston Grove

200

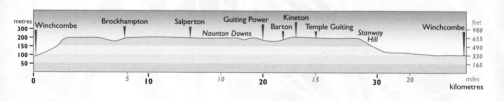

metres		Winchcombe	Brockhampton	Salperton		Guiting Power	Kineton		Temple Guiting	Stanway Hill	Winchcombe	feet
300					Naunton Downs		Barton				980
200											655
150											490
100											330
50											165

0   5   10   15   20   30   miles
          10   15   20   30   kilometres

THE SOUTHERN END – LANSDOWN, DYRHAM AND BATHEASTON

Route information

Distance 43.5km (27 miles)

Grade Strenuous

Terrain The route is mostly on unclassified roads, some narrow and twisting, with both flat and hilly sections. There are two steep descents.

Time to allow 3-5 hours.

Getting there by car On top of Lansdown Hill, above Bath and just south of the racecourse, is a Park and Ride car park, open weekdays only, and wide grass verges where you can leave a vehicle. Lansdown car park can be reached from Bath by way of Lansdown Hill. If travelling

from the north, on the A46, take RHF about 5km (3 miles) south of the M4, following signs to Park and Ride. An alternative would be to start the ride at Marshfield, just off the A420 between Bristol and Chippenham. There is some parking in the town and ample car parking space where the route joins the A420 at direction 8.

Getting there by train Bath is on the main railway line between Bristol and Swindon. The station is about 5km (3 miles) from the car park at Lansdown. This is a long climb and the train traveller might prefer to start the circuit at Batheaston, (direction 12), also about 5km (3 miles) from Bath station, but on the flat.

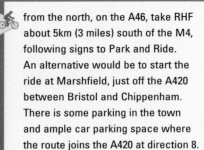

From Lansdown Hill, down into the Cotswold scarp and back up again beyond Dyrham. The route then takes you across the wolds, eventually turning south to follow the Foss Way for a few kilometres before descending to Batheaston. There follows an undulating lane winding through the St Catherine valley and back to Lansdown Hill. There was an important battle near Dyrham, when in 577 the Saxons gained control of Gloucester, Cirencester and Bath. The actual site of the battle was Hinton Hill, just to the north of Dyrham.

Places of interest along the route

A Lansdown Monument, Lansdown Hill

As the road across the flat top of Lansdown Hill begins to descend northwards towards Doynton, a track leads off to the right. A few metres along the track is a monument surmounted by a griffin. Although the monument is to the memory of Sir Bevil Grenville, a Royalist officer killed during the

Battle of Lansdown Hill, it serves as a marker of the actual battle. Fought on 5 July 1643, the battle was a victory for the Royalists.

B Dyrham Park, Dyrham

Dyrham Park, covering an area of 107 hectares (264 acres), is owned by the National Trust. Dyrham House, built by William Blathwayt, Secretary of State to William III, is a fine example of 17th-century interior decorating and furnishing. Deer, which gave Dyrham its name, can still be seen in the deer park and there are panoramic views to the south west. Gardens and restaurant. The house is open daily from April to October (except Wednesday-Thursday) 1200-1730; the garden is open from April to October (except Wednesday-Thursday) 1100-1730; and the park is open daily, all year round, 1200-1730 (or dusk if earlier). Charge. Telephone the house on (0117) 9372501 and the park on (01225) 891364.

Food and drink

There is a restaurant at Dyrham Park serving coffee, lunches and teas.

Cross House Inn, Doynton
On the left as you go through the village. Home cooked lunches available every day.

Crown Inn, Marshfield
This old coaching inn is on the left of the main street in Marshfield. Meals served and take-aways also available.

Shoe Inn, on A420 east of Marshfield
The pub has a restaurant serving steaks and grills.

Northend Inn, Batheaston
On the left in Batheaston, as the route bends northwards. Good food and bar snacks.

Three Shire Stone

Lansdown Monument

Route description

Leave the car park and TL, heading in a north westerly direction.

1 Arrive A420 XR and SO, SP Doynton and Dyrham. **6km (3.5 miles)**

2 TJ TR SP Bath, Stroud and Marshfield. **10.5km (6.5 miles)**

3 TJ TL SP 13th-century church. To visit Dyrham Park TR at TJ and then TL at A46 – the entrance is a short way along.

4 TR opposite Talbot Farm (no SP) and climb to the top of the Cotswold scarp.

5 TR (no SP).

6 At XR with A46, SO SP West Littleton. **14km (8.5 miles)**

7 XR with A420, SO (no SP) into Marshfield (18km/11 miles). Go down Touching End Lane and TL onto Main Street. TL then TR.

Dyrham House

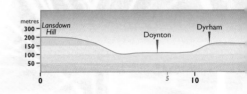

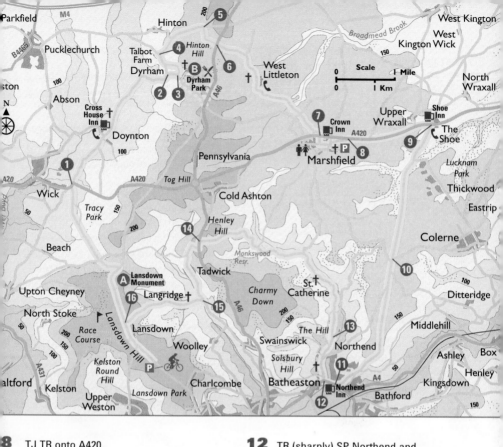

8 TJ TR onto A420.

9 XR at the Shoe Inn, TR SP Colerne.

10 Staggered XR, SO SP Ditteridge, Box and Bath (24.5km/15 miles). After approximately 0.5km, look for the Three Shire Stones (they look like small standing stones) on the right – this point was originally the cornerstone of Gloucestershire, Wiltshire and Somerset.

11 At foot of long steep descent, TJ TR.

12 TR (sharply) SP Northend and St Catherine. **30km (18.5 miles)**

13 Take LHF SP St Catherine's Church.

14 TJ (A46) TL. Then, after 150m, TR SP Tadwick. **37.5km (23.5 miles)**

15 TR SP Langridge.

16 TJ TL and return to Lansdown car park. Or, if you started the route at Marshfield or Batheaston, TR. **43.5km (27 miles)**

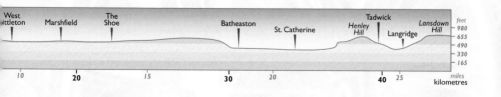

STOW-ON-THE-WOLD, BOURTON, WINDRUSH AND BLEDINGTON

Route information

Distance   46km (28.5 miles)

Grade   Strenuous

Terrain   A downhill start, across the undulating countryside south of Stow and two hills to climb. Two stretches of the route use bridleways, which can get muddy in wet weather.

Time to allow   3-4 hours.

Getting there by car   Stow is on the A429 (the Foss Way), about 12.5km (8 miles) north of Northleach. There is a car park with toilets on the A436 about 0.5km (0.3 miles) from the A429 as it goes through the town.

Getting there by train   Shipton Station is approximately 3km (2 miles) east of Milton-under-Wychwood (direction17); Kingham Station is around 0.5km (0.3 miles) east of the junction between Foscot and Bledington (direction 21). For information telephone (0345) 484950.

This route takes you from Stow-on-the-Wold down to Bourton, up and down through the Windrush valley to the Barringtons. Then the route follows single track lanes before turning north to Milton. From there two separate sections of bridleway take you to the final climb up to Stow. The route is generally rural, with good spots for picnics.

Places of interest along the route

🅐 Stow-on-the-Wold

Stow-on-the-Wold is the highest Cotswold town at 244m (800 feet), giving rise to the rhyme 'Stow on the Wold where the wind blows cold'. Great sheep fairs were held here, with up to 20,000 sheep being marketed at one time. The narrow streets of Stow created passages through which the sheep could easily be directed.

🅑 Bourton-on-the-Water

Bourton, the site of a settlement since pre-Roman times, is always busy with visitors and there is plenty to see and do. **The Model Village** is a replica of Bourton itself, built of local stone at one-ninth scale. Open daily, in the summer 0900-1600 and in the winter 1000-1600. Charge. Telephone (01451) 820467. **Birdland** has a wide variety of tropical and non-tropical birds, together with a picnic area, children's play area, gardens and cafeteria. Open from March to October 1000-1800; from November to February 1000-1600. Charge. Telephone (01451) 820480. **Bourton Model Railway** is one of the finest indoor model railway layouts in the country. Over 40 British and Continental trains run automatically through imaginative scenery. There is a model and toy shop. Open daily from April to September 1100-1730; from October to March at weekends only 1100-1700. Charge. Telephone (01451) 820686. The **Cotswold Motor Museum and Toy Collection** has cars, motorcycles, pedal-powered vehicles, caravans, a magnificent collection of memorabilia, period advertising signs and a childhood toy collection. Open daily from February to November 1000-1800. Charge. Telephone (01451) 821255. The **Cotswold Perfumery** is a unique experience and the only exhibition of its kind in Europe – an audio 'smelly-vision' display, an ingredients room, perfume quiz and perfumed garden. Gift shop. Open daily (except Christmas Day and Boxing Day) Monday to Saturday 0930-1700, Sunday 1030-1700. Charge for admission to exhibition. Telephone (01451) 820698.

ⓒ Windrush Church, Windrush

Delightful Norman church in the centre of the village. Usually open. Admission free.

ⓓ Bledington Church, Bledington

This church is famous for its Perpendicular windows and stained glass. The earlier part of the church, including the nave, is 12th century and the chancel is Early English. Usually open with free admission.

Food and drink

Stow and Bourton have numerous pubs, cafés and tearooms.

Golden Ball, Lower Swell.
Real ales and bar snacks available.

Old Farmhouse Hotel, Lower Swell
Morning coffee, bar snacks and teas.

Fox Inn, Little Barrington
Coffee (from 1100), real ales and bar snacks available.

Quart Pot, Milton-under-Wychwood
On your right, just before the route turns left in the village – bar snacks served.

King's Head Inn, Bledington
Morning coffee (from 1100), real ales and bar snacks.

Stow-on-the-Wold

Route description

From the car park, go up to the through road and TL along Park Street (becomes Sheep Street) to the traffic lights. SO onto B4068, SP Lower Swell.

1 SP the Slaughters TL.

2 SP Upper Slaughter TR, along an undulating lane.

3 Arrive Upper Slaughter and TR, just before the river, along road SP Unsuitable for Motors to the ford. *5.5km (3.5 miles)*

4 SO through the ford, up the hill and at the through road TR.

5 SP Bourton TL, then TR SP Bourton.

6 SP Bourton-on-the-Water TL.

7 At A429 TJ TR (with care) then immediately TL along Lansdown into Bourton. *9km (5.5 miles)*

8 In Bourton TR along Sherborne Street (just before the greens begin). Climb ahead outside Bourton.

9 TL SP Sherborne. *15.5km (9.5 miles)*

10 XR SP Windrush TL. Go through Sherborne and along a quiet lane through the Windrush Valley.

11 TL TJ SP Great Barrington, over the River Windrush and up to Great Barrington. *22km (13.5 miles)*

12 TR in Great Barrington, SP Taynton.

13 TL SP Milton-Under-Wychwood and along single track road. *27.5km (17 miles)*

14 A424 XR SO (no sign), and continue along single track road.

15 TJ SP Milton-under-Wychwood TL, then left again, also SP Milton-under-Wychwood.

16 Upper Milton XR SO, SP Milton-under-Wychwood. *31.5km (19.5 miles)*

17 TL SP Kingham.

18 TJ SP Bruern, TR.

19 TL just before the wood (no sign). The tarmac becomes uneven track. There is usually a field of handsome Jacobs sheep along here. Soon after the houses the road becomes tarmac again. *36.5km (22.5 miles)*

20 Foscot TJ TR (no SP).

21 B4450 TJ, SP Bledington, TL and into the village. The green is on the far side of Bledington.

22 TL SP Icomb. *41km (25.5 miles)*

23 TL SP Icomb.

24 SO SP Icomb. TR at War Memorial and follow the road round and up the hill.

25 TJ SP Bledington TR, then first left (no SP). *43.5km (27 miles)*

26 As the road bends left, go SO onto bridleway. There are lovely views of Stow church ahead. The route goes downhill and then uphill onto tarmac.

27 TJ TR (no SP) into Maugersbury.

28 TJ TR (no SP), then immediately TL SP Stow-on-the-Wold, past a telephone box. Continue along this road to the car park and the end of the route. *46km (28.5 miles)*

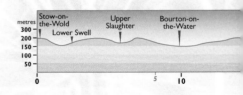

Upper Swell

Adlestrop

Lower Oddington

Daylesford

200

Old Farmhouse Hotel

Stow-on-the-Wold

A

Lower Swell

① Golden Ball

A436

Upper Oddington

Kingham

Churchill

P ② ⑧

⑦

Maugersbury

150

N

②

Dismantled railway

ford Hill

③

Copse Hill

R. Dikler

Foss Way

Maugersbury Hill ⑯

B4450

② ②

⑨ ⑨

④ 禾

⑤ Upper Slaughter

A424

② ⑦

Icomb

② ⑨

King's Head ⑨

Bledington ⑨

Foscot

Sars Brook

⑥

Lower Slaughter

⑦ ⑧

Wyck Rissington

② ②

禾 ⑨

Westcote Brook

D ⑨

②①

⑧ Motor Museum Model Railway

Bourton-on-the-Water

B

⑨ ⑨

Church Westcote

Bould

Lyneham

Cotswold Perfumery Birdland

Model Village

Little Rissington

Nether Westcote

⑨

⑨ Bruern Wood

Idbury

⑯

A429

Clapton-on-the-Hill

Fifield

Milton-under-Wychwood

⑰

oxhill

⑨

River Windrush

Great Rissington

200

Tangley Woods

Quart Pot

Shipton-under-Wychwood

150

Farmington Grove

Taynton Bushes

Upper Milton

Blenheim

Sherborne Common

Horseclose Copse

Habber Gallows Hill

⑯

B4437

150

Sherborne

Brook

Sherborne

Hazelford Brook

A424

150

⑩

Sherborne Park

Deer Park

⑭

Fulbrook Gap

Widley Copse

A40

⑪

Windrush

⑫ Great Barrington

⑮

Fulbrook

A361

Scale 1 Mile

Fox Inn

Taynton

⑬

Westhall Hill

0 1 Km

ge k

Budgehill Wood

† C

Little Barrington

Upton

A40

B4425

Burford

Swinbrook Widford

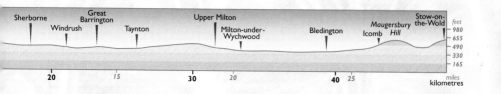

Sherborne | Great Barrington | Upper Milton | Stow-on-the-Wold

feet 980

Windrush | Milton-under-Wychwood | Bledington | Icomb | Maugersbury Hill

655
490
330
165

20 15 30 20 40 25

miles

kilometres

CIRENCESTER, CHEDWORTH, NORTHLEACH AND BARNSLEY

Route information

Distance 47km (29 miles)

Grade Moderate

Terrain A demanding hill out of Chedworth, otherwise gentle country lanes and a short stretch of A road on the return to Cirencester.

Time to allow 3-6 hours.

Getting there by car Cirencester is on the A429 from Stow-on-the-Wold; the A419 from Stroud; and the A417 from Lechlade. The Phoenix car park on London Road, Cirencester would be a convenient car park for this route.

Getting there by train There is a railway station at Kemble, about 4.5km (3 miles) south west of Cirencester. For information telephone (0345) 484950.

From Cirencester, the Roman town of Corinium, along the Roman White Way to Chedworth and its Roman villa, and then on to Northleach and Barnsley. The route around the Roman villa is the most strenuous part of the ride. The countryside is rolling sheep pasture, the source of the wealth that built the church and big houses in Northleach. From Northleach you ride south over the Coln River to Barnsley, a beautiful stone village with a famous garden. The last two miles of the route follow the A417 – a fairly quiet road – back into Cirencester.

Places of interest along the route

Ⓐ Corinium Museum, Cirencester

The Corinium Museum, based in Roman Britain's second largest town, holds much more than a fine collection of Roman antiquities. There is a gallery on the Roman military, a reconstructed Roman dining room and kitchen, a Roman butcher's shop and garden, as well as beautiful mosaic floors and wall paintings. The museum follows and explains Cotswold history from prehistory to the English Civil War and beyond: Iron Age, Saxon and Medieval galleries and features on the wool trade. Open daily throughout the year (except Mondays from November to March), Monday-Saturday 1000-1700, Sunday 1400-1700. Charge. Telephone (01285) 655611.

Ⓑ Chedworth Roman Villa, Yanworth

This National Trust property is one of the best exposed Romano British villas in Britain. It was, in fact, a Roman country mansion and outbuildings, situated in a sheltered valley. The lower parts of many of the buildings have been exposed and there is plenty to see including a water shrine and spring, two bath houses and fine 4th-century mosaics. An on-site museum explains the history of the villa. Open from March to October, Tuesday-Sunday and Bank Holidays 1000-1700; during November, Tuesday-Sunday 1000-1600. Charge. Telephone (01242) 890256.

Ⓒ Northleach Church, Northleach

Northleach Church is considered to be one of the finest Cotswold wool churches – wealth wool merchants financed its rebuilding during the 15th century. It contains a famous collection of wool merchants' brasses. Open daily throughout the year. Admission free.

D Cotswold Countryside Collection, Northleach

This museum of country life is housed in the remaining buildings of the Northleach House of Correction, built in 1791 and one of the country prisons of Gloucestershire. There is a restored cell block and 19th-century courtroom. The museum contains examples of the crafts and tools necessary to rural life, harvest wagons and other horse-drawn vehicles. There is a history of farming, from prehistoric through to Victorian times and an exhibition recreating a laundry, kitchen and dairy in the days before labour-saving devices. Tearoom and picnic area. Open daily from April to October, Monday-Saturday 1000-1700, Sunday 1400-1700. Charge. Telephone (01451) 860715.

E Keith Harding's World of Mechanical Music, Northleach

Billed as a 'unique experience in sound', this award-winning museum displays all manner of musical boxes, self-playing instruments and clocks, maintained on the premises. Listen to concert performances from Grieg, Rachmaninov and Gershwin; a 1920s Berlin café piano; a 1930s gramophone; and experience a Victorian music room. Guided tours include demonstrations of all types of organs, pianos, musical boxes and gramophones. Gift shop and antique clocks and musical boxes for sale. Open daily all year round (except Christmas Day) 1000-1800. Charge. Telephone (01451) 860181.

F Barnsley House Gardens, Barnsley

Magnificent gardens owned and developed by Rosemary Verey, the well-known writer on English gardens. They feature spring bulbs and autumn colour, mixed borders, climbing and wall shrubs, vegetable, knot and herb gardens, a Laburnum walk, 18th-century summer houses and a decorative vegetable potager. Open Monday, Wednesday, Thursday and Saturday throughout the year 1000-1800. Charge. Telephone (01285) 740281.

Food and drink

There are many pubs, hotels and tearooms in Cirencester and several pubs in Northleach.

Seven Tuns, Chedworth
On the right as you go through the village, serving real ales and bar snacks.

Corner Green Restaurant and Tea Shop, Northleach
On the right, out of Market Square, opposite Keith Harding's World of Mechanical Music – coffee, lunches and teas.

Village Pub, Barnsley
On the B4425 in Barnsley. Morning coffee (from 1100), real ales and bar snacks.

Crown of Crucis, Ampney Crucis
On the left before direction 23. Morning coffee, bar snacks and teas available.

Route description

From St John Baptist's church, Cirencester, TR along West Market Place, Gosditch Street and Dollar Street. At end of Dollar Street, TR into Spitalgate Lane.

1 XR SO onto the White Way.
4km (2.5 miles)

2 TR SP Calmsden.

3 TJ SP Chedworth, TR into Calmsden – notice the estate cottages on the right.
7.5km (5 miles)

4 TL SP Chedworth.

5 SO XR SP Yanworth.

6 TL at TJ SP Yanworth, into the centre of Chedworth. *11.5km (7 miles)*

7 TR SP Roman Villa, at first downhill, then steeply uphill.

8 TL at XR SP Roman Villa.

9 TJ SP Roman Villa, TL. *18km (11 miles)*

10 On leaving the Roman Villa, go back along road you arrived on, SP Yanworth and TL at junction.

11 SP Northleach TR. *23.5km (14.5 miles)*

12 SO SP Northleach.

13 SO at A429, SP Mill End – the lane is named All Alone.

14 TJ TL, down the hill and over Mill View bridge. TR into Church Walk and TL into Northleach Market Place to visit the church, museum and World of Mechanical Music. Leave Northleach by retracing your route.
25km (15.5 miles

15 SO SP Ablington.

16 SO at XR, SP Coln St. Dennis.

17 TJ SP Coln St. Dennis, TR into the village TL SP Coln Rogers. *31.5km (19.5 miles)*

18 TR (no SP) just before the river – climb ahead.

19 SO at XR, SP Barnsley.

20 TL at B4425 XR, SP Barnsley. Return to XR at B4425 to continue ride.
37km (23 miles)

21 TL SP Ampney Crucis.

22 TR SP Ampney Crucis. There is a shop here. *41.5km (26 miles)*

23 TR at A417 XR, SP Cirencester.

24 Arrive Cirencester: TL into Churchill Way TR into Whitelands Road; TL into Upperside Churnside; TR over bridge and along Beeches Way, back to the Phoenix car park.
47km (29 miles

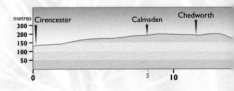

N

Withington

Cassey
Compton

R. Coln

Star Wood

Withington
Woods

Yanworth
Wood

Yanworth

Chedworth
Roman
Villa

B

11

Stowell
Grove

Cotswold
Countryside
Collection

D

World of
Mechanical
Music

Mill End

E

Northleach

12

Farmington

C †

14

Corner
Green
Restaurant

Chedworth Woods

10

9

13

15

A40

olesbourne
Park

olesbourne

Chedworth
Laines

7

☎

🏠 Chedworth

8

Stowell

Eastington

Penhill
Plantation

en
ill

A435

Seven
Tuns

6

Stowell
Park

16

Fossebridge

Eycot
Wood

5

Lower
Chedworth

Foss Way

Coln
St. Dennis

17

150

Rendcomb
Park

Rendcomb

4

Calmsden

3

Foss
Cross

19

18

Calcot

Coln Rogers

Winson

Ablington

200

North
Cerney

Woodmancote

R. Churn

White Way

A429

Barnsley
Wood

150

Arlington

Bibury

B4425

River Coln

Bagendon

150

Perrott's
Brook

2

Dismantled railway

Wiggold

Village
Pub

F

Barnsley
House Gardens

Barnsley

20

21

Ready Token

Daglingworth

Baunton

Stratton

1

Corinium
Museum

A

B4425

Ampney
Crucis

Sunhill

22

Ampney
St. Mary

Scale

0   1 Mile

irencester Park

A417

🚲 †

P

24

Cirencester

🏠 ✕ ☕

Preston

23

Crown
of Crucis

Ampney
St. Peter

Poulton

100

0   1 Km

A419

Chesterton

A419

A433

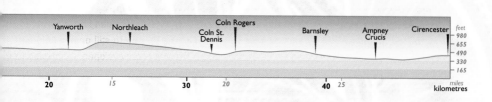

Yanworth

Northleach

Coln Rogers

Coln St.
Dennis

Barnsley

Ampney
Crucis

Cirencester

feet
980
655
490
330
165

20

15

30

40

25

miles
kilometres

CHIPPING CAMPDEN AND COTSWOLD GARDENS

Route information

Distance 57km (35.5 miles)

Grade Strenuous

Terrain Narrow country lanes through the undulating countryside north of Stow-on-the-Wold – there are some steep hills.

Time to allow 4 hours.

Getting there by car Lower Swell is 1.5km (1 mile) west of Stow-on-the-Wold, on the B4068. You can park on the roadside.

Getting there by train There are no convenient rail links to the start of this route.

From Lower Swell to Snowshill, Chipping Campden, Hidcote and back through Batsford. This lovely ride is over high upland countryside north of Stow-on-the-Wold. It goes over open farmland and through wooded areas and passes three beautiful gardens. Chipping Campden is one of the most lovely Cotswold towns, with well preserved buildings; it was a centre of the early 19th-century Cotswold Arts and Crafts movement. Note that it is extremely busy in the north Cotswolds during summer weekends.

Places of interest along the route

Ⓐ Snowshill Manor, Snowshill

A National Trust property, this Cotswold manor house contains Charles Wade's fascinating collection of craftmanship from all over the world, displayed by theme – from navigation to musical instruments and Samurai armour. Cottage gardens, restaurant and gift shop. Open daily (except Tuesday) from April to October 1200-1700; during July and August open every day. Charge. Telephone (01386) 852410.

Ⓑ Broadway Tower and Country Park

The Tower – a folly – was built in 1800 by the Earl of Coventry who lived about 32km (20 miles) north of its location. The tower is 312m (1024 feet) above sea level and on a fine day 14 counties can be seen from the top. The Country Park has exhibitions in the Tower and the nearby barn, a woodland nature walk, a picnic area, shop and refreshments. Open daily from April to October 1000-1800. Charge Telephone (01386) 852390.

Ⓒ Dover's Hill, near Chipping Campden

In the care of the National Trust, Dover's Hill covers 75 hectares (185 acres) of open grassland and woods. There are panoramic views of the Vale of Evesham. The hill was the site of the 17th-century Olympics of rural sports, which included cudgels, slingsticks and shin kicking. There are still games held here in June. The site is always open. Admission free.

D **Kiftsgate Court Gardens,**
near Chipping Campden

Many rare shrubs and plants (including *Kiftsgate*, the largest English rose), enclosed in a series of retaining walls. Plants for sale. Teas available from June to August. Open from April to September, Wednesday, Thursday and Sunday 1400-1800. Charge. Telephone (01386) 438777.

E **Hidcote Manor Garden,**
near Chipping Campden

These beautiful world famous gardens comprise a series of smaller gardens. National Trust owned. Shop, plant sales and restaurant. Open daily (except Tuesday and Friday) from April to October; daily in June and July (except Friday). From April to September 1100-1800, during October 1100-1700. Charge. Telephone (01386) 438333.

F **Sezincote House and Gardens,**
near Longborough

An oriental water garden surrounds a rococo mansion built in Moorish style. The house is open Thursday-Friday during May, June, July and September 1430-1800. The gardens are open Thursday-Friday all year round, except December, 1400-1800. Charge.

Food and drink

There are many pubs, restaurants and tearooms in Chipping Campden. The following serve morning coffee, bar snacks and real ales: The Plough, Ford; Snowshill Arms, Snowshill; Ebrington Arms, Ebrington; Churchill Inn, Paxford (continue along B4479 at direction 23; the inn is on the left).

Old Farmhouse Hotel, Lower Swell
Coffee, bar snacks, restaurant and teas.

Golden Ball, Lower Swell
Real ales and bar snacks.

Coach and Horses Inn, Longborough
Village pub serving real ales.

Hidcote Manor Garden

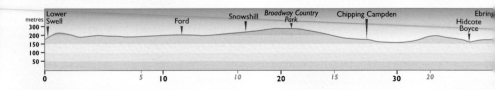

elevation profile with labels: Lower Swell, Ford, Snowshill, Broadway Country Park, Chipping Campden, Ebring(ton) Hidcote Boyce; metres axis 300, 200, 150, 100, 50; distance markers 0, 5, 10, 10, 20, 15, 30, 20

Route description

From Lower Swell, head west along the B4068 and bear right SP Guiting Power.
6km (3.5 miles)

1 At XR TR SP Snowshill.

2 Arrive B4077 XR. TL, SP Ford, and downhill to the village. **12km (7.5 miles)**

3 XR (no SP) TR and follow signs to Snowshill.

4 TL SP Snowshill and into the village. You will pass Snowshill Manor on your left.
17km (10.5 miles)

5 TR out of Snowshill Manor, then take LHF SP Chipping Campden.

6 TL XR (no SP).

7 TL XR SP Chipping Campden.

8 TL TJ SP Chipping Campden.

9 TL SP Broadway and along a wooded lane. You will pass Broadway Tower and Country Park on the left. **22km (13.5 miles)**

10 Arrive A44 XR. SO SP Saintbury. Keep right at XR.

11 XR. TL for Dover's Hill or TR and down-hill into Chipping Campden. Leave Chipping Campden on the B4081, SP Mickleton.
27km (17 miles)

12 TR SP Hidcote.

13 TR SP Hidcote Gardens.

14 SP Unsuitable for Motors TL.

15 TL at TJ (no SP).

16 Kiftsgate Court is to the left. TR to Hidcote Manor Garden. **33km (20.5 miles)**

17 Retrace your route to direction 15 and go SO.

18 SO XR SP Ebrington.

19 Ebrington TJ, bear left into the village.

20 TR at Ebrington Arms, SP Paxford.
38.5km (24 miles)

21 SO at B4035 XR, SP Paxford.

22 TR at B4479 TJ, SP Paxford.

23 In Paxford TL, SP Aston Magna, and then TL again.

24 TR Aston Magna TJ, SP Blockley and up the hill. **43.5km (27 miles)**

25 TL, SP Batsford, and continue uphill.

26 In Batsford TR SP Blockley.

27 Arrive B4479 TJ and TL, SP Bourton-on-the-Hill. **48.5km (30 miles)**

28 At A44, TL SP Oxford. To visit Batsford Arboretum, continue left along A44.

29 TR SP Longborough. You will pass Sezincote House and Gardens on the left.

30 TL TJ SP Longborough.
52.5km (32.5 miles)

31 TR in Longborough, SP Stow-on-the-Wold.

32 At A424 TJ, TL SP Stow.

33 TR SP Upper Swell.

34 TL SP Upper Swell and go down the hill, passing Donnington Brewery on the right.

35 At B4077 TJ TL, SP Stow.

36 TR SP Lower Swell, and return to the start of the route. **57km (35.5 miles)**

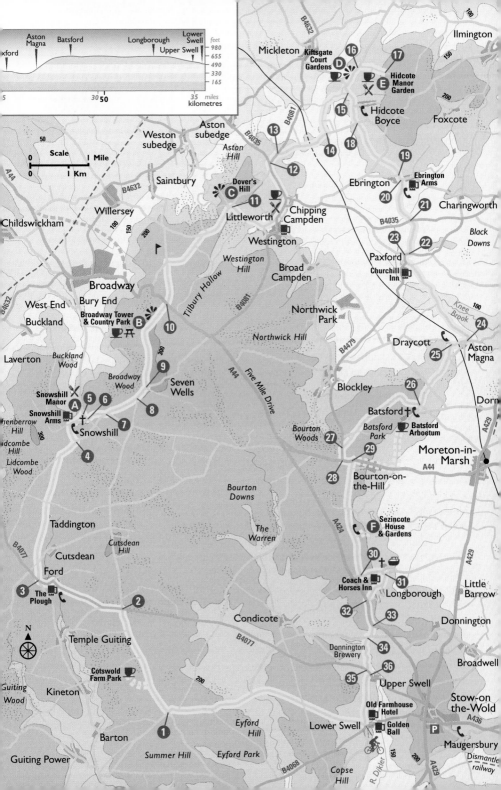

Map labels and locations

Ilmington

Mickleton

Kiftsgate Court Gardens **D**

16

17 Hidcote Manor Garden **E**

Foxcote

15 Hidcote Boyce

13

14 **18**

19 Ebrington Arms

Ebrington **20**

Charingworth

21

Aston subedge

Aston Hill

12

Weston subedge

Saintbury

Dover's Hill **C**

11 Littleworth

Chipping Campden

Westington

Westington Hill

Broad Campden

Black Downs

23 Paxford

22

Childswickham

Willersey

Broadway

Bury End West End

Buckland

Broadway Tower & Country Park **B**

10

Tilbury Hollow

Northwick Park

Northwick Hill

Five Mile Drive

Churchill Inn

Knee Brook

Draycott

24

25

Aston Magna

Dorn

Laverton

Buckland Wood

Broadway Wood

9

Seven Wells

8

Snowshill Manor **A**

5 **6**

Snowshill Arms

7 Snowshill

4

Henberrow Hill *Lidcombe Hill* *Lidcombe Wood*

Blockley

26

Batsford Batsford Arboretum

Batsford Park

Bourton Woods

27

29

Bourton-on-the-Hill

28

Moreton-in-Marsh

Bourton Downs

Taddington

Cutsdean Hill

Cutsdean

Ford

3 The Plough

2

The Warren

Sezincote House & Gardens **F**

30

Coach & Horses Inn

31 Longborough

32

Little Barrow

Donnington

Condicote

Donnington Brewery

33

34

Broadwell

36

35 Upper Swell

Stow-on-the-Wold

N

Temple Guiting

Cotswold Farm Park

Kineton

Guiting Wood

Eyford Hill

Eyford Park

1

Summer Hill

Barton

Guiting Power

Old Farmhouse Hotel

Lower Swell

Golden Ball

Maugersbury

Copse Hill

Dismantled railway

R. Dikler

Elevation profile (inset)

xford — Aston Magna — Batsford — Longborough — Upper Swell — Lower Swell

feet: 980, 655, 490, 330, 165

5 — 30 — 50 — 35 *miles* kilometres

Scale (inset)

Scale

0 — 1 Mile

0 — 1 Km

Route information

Distance 61km (38 miles)

Grade Moderate

Terrain Mostly unclassified roads, some narrow, a few climbs of reasonable gradient and two steep descents.

Time to allow 4-6 hours.

Getting there by car Tetbury is south of Stroud on the B4014 and on the A433, south west of Cirencester. There are several car parks in Tetbury.

Getting there by train Kemble is the nearest station, about 14.5km (9 miles) from Tetbury.

From Tetbury, south as far as the village of Biddestone, returning to Tetbury through Great and Little Badminton and Westonbirt. This ride, for the most part, takes you over the broad flat top of the Cotswolds. Only at the southern end of the circuit (around the middle part of the route) do well-defined hills and valleys become features of the landscape. There are hills to be climbed but they are mostly short distances – even around Slaughterford and Castle Combe there are no long uphill slogs. However, there are two extremely steep descents. River valley scenery can be enjoyed at Easton Grey, Slaughterford, Ford and Castle Combe; Biddestone, Castle Combe and Great Badminton are the pick of the villages. Castle Combe is a well known tourist centre and can become quite crowded. There are no television

ariels here, a legacy of the filming of Doctor Doolittle *some years ago. At Great Badminton, a partial circuit of the village takes you past the entrance to the Great House (not open to the public), dating from 1682 and remodelled in 1740, and the seat of the Duke of Beaufort. Badminton, of course, is the venue for the well-known annual three-day horse trials.*

Places of interest along the route

A Tetbury Police Museum, Tetbury
The museum is housed in the original cells of the old police station and contains many artefacts from the Gloucestershire Constabulary. Open from March to October, Monday-Saturday 1015-1615. Admission free. Telephone (01666) 503552 for further information.

B Westonbirt Arboretum, Tetbury
Westonbirt Arboretum is run by Forest Enterprise. The first planting took place in 1829 and today there are over 18,000 trees, from all over the world, covering an area of 243 hectares (600 acres) with miles of waymarked trails. The arboretum is full of wildlife and is a magnificent place at any time of year: from March to June you can see displays of rhododendrons, azaleas, magnolias and many wild flowers; during the summer the Lime Avenue hums to the sound of bees and you will see plenty of butterflies; the autumn colour is spectacular; and in winter the cherries, birches and dogwoods show off coloured stems. Visitor centre, gift shop, plant centre, courtyard café and picnic areas. Open daily all year round 1000-2000, or sunset when earlier. Charge. Telephone (01666) 880220.

Food and drink

Tetbury has numerous hotels, pubs and cafés and there are pubs and cafés in Castle Combe. Refreshments are available at Westonbirt Arboretum.

✗ Two Toads Restaurant, Church Street, Tetbury
Open Monday-Saturday 0900-1630, Sunday 1000-1700 for coffee, lunches and teas.

Cat & Custard Pot, Shipton Moyne
On your right as you go through the village. Morning coffee and bar snacks are available.

White Horse Inn, Biddestone
Beside the village green – a salubrious spot to sit and eat or drink on a summer's day. Home cooked food is served and the pub is open all day on Saturdays and Sundays.

White Hart Inn, Ford
Built in 1553, this building is listed as being of architectural and historic interest. Morning coffee, extensive menu and real ales available.

The Gates, Castle Combe
Teashop serving coffee, lunches and teas. Closed on Mondays.

Rattlebone Inn, Sherston
16th-century building in Sherston's main street. The pub owes its name to a local hero who fought in the Battle of Sherston in 1016. It has an unusual six-sided pool table. Real ales and hot and cold meals.

Westonbirt Arboretum

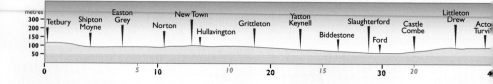

metres
300
200
150
100
50
0

Tetbury Shipton Moyne Easton Grey Norton New Town Hullavington Grittleton Yatton Keynell Biddestone Slaughterford Ford Castle Combe Littleton Drew Acton Turvi*

0   5 10   10   20   15   30   20   4

Route description

From the Market Hall in the centre of Tetbury, cycle south down Church Street (the A433).

1 TL SP Shipton Moyne.

2 Arrive Shipton Moyne. Go through the village and TR, SP Easton Grey.
4km (2.5 miles)

3 SO XR with B4040. Descend through Easton Grey to a bridge across the River Avon.

4 At Norton TR and then TL, SP Hullavington.
10km (6 miles)

5 Shortly after railway bridge, TR SP Hullavington and Grittleton and go through Hullavington village.

6 In Grittleton village, at XR TL, SP Yatton Keynell.
18km (11 miles)

7 2.5km (1.5 miles) after passing over the M4 motorway, arrive Yatton Keynell. Join B4039, pass Bell Inn and take RHF by post office/shop, SP Biddestone.
22km (13.5 miles)

8 Cross the A420 and enter Biddestone village. At TJ TL to see the village. Return to the TJ and go SO SP Hartham. Pass the diminutive church to the right then RHF into Challows Lane – it is easy to go wrong here.
25.5km (16 miles)

9 After descending steeply through woods with care – the road is narrow with a loose surface – cross the By Brook (ignore left turn). Pass Slaughterford Church and TL up a hill.

10 The lane climbs and then descends steeply to Ford. At TJ TR, then TR along the A420. TL SP Castle Combe.
29.5km (18.5 miles)

11 RHF SP Castle Combe and descend through the village. At junction TL onto B4039.

12 1km (0.5 miles) after passing the Salutation Inn on the B4039, TR SP Littleton Drew, and go under the M4 motorway.
35.5km (22 miles)

13 Go through Littleton Drew. Arrive Acton Turville and TR (by old pump house) SP Badminton.

14 TR to go round the village of Great Badminton, passing the entrance to Badminton House (not open to the public).
40km (25 miles)

15 After passing through Little Badminton, TR through a gateway opposite a house. In spite of its appearance and the Footpath SP, this is a public road. After the gateway follow the road round to the left. Badminton Park is on your right.

16 At TJ TR.
45.5km (28.5 miles)

17 Enter Sherston and TR at XR then join the B4040 opposite the Rattlebone Inn. TL through Sherston and at XR TL, SP Westonbirt and Tetbury.

18 At XR TL to comply with one-way system (Westonbirt village is to the right). Almost immediately, TR along the A433. A short distance further, a driveway to the left leads to Westonbirt Arboretum.
54.5 km (34 miles)

19 TL (no SP).

20 At XR TR along A4135. Enter Tetbury and at main XR TR to return to the Market Hall.
61km (38 miles)

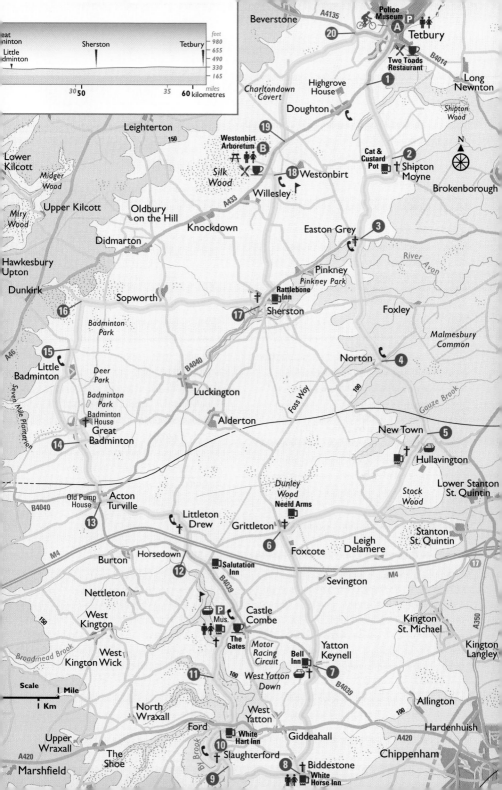

MORETON-IN-MARSH TO THE ROLLRIGHT STONES

Route information

Distance 62.5km (39 miles)

Grade Moderate

Terrain Mostly through farming country on unclassified roads. There are a number of climbs, none of them major.

Time to allow 4-5 hours.

Getting there by car Moreton-in-Marsh is on the A429 (the Roman Foss Way). Car parking is signposted but if no spaces are available it is possible to park in the lane towards Batsford.

Getting there by train There is a railway station at the north end of Moreton's High Street. This is on a secondary line between Worcester and Oxford. Telephone (0345) 484950 for information.

A tour of Cotswold villages (12 in all) and two of the Cotswolds' principal towns – Chipping Norton and Stow-on-the-Wold – in a circuit starting from Moreton-in-Marsh. The route touches three counties – Gloucestershire, Oxfordshire and Warwickshire – and passes the Rollright Stones, prehistoric relics, from where there are marvellous panoramic views.

Places of interest along the route

A Moreton-in-Marsh

Standing alongside Moreton's High Street, which is on the line of the Roman Foss Way, is a quaint stone tower with a bell turret. The structure is medieval and the bell used to be rung to herald the curfew. The clock is 17th century. A popular market is held in Moreton on Tuesdays.

B Rollright Stones, between Great and Little Rollright

The Rollright Stones, prehistoric standing stones, are next only to Stonehenge and Avebury in importance. The main circle (the King's Men) is 30.5m (100 feet) across and some of the stones stand 2m (7 feet) high. Across a field is a smaller group of stones known as the Whispering Knights, and on the opposite side of the road is the King's Stone, now protected by railings. The origin of the stones is believed to be earlier than 1500BC. The stones are accessible at all times and a donation is requested.

C Stow-on-the-Wold

Stow-on-the-Wold is the highest Cotswold town at 244m (800 feet), giving rise to the rhyme 'Stow on the Wold where the wind blows cold'. Great sheep fairs were held here, with up to 20,000 sheep being marketed at one time. Many old buildings survive and are clustered around the Market Place.

Little Rollright

Food and drink

There is a wide choice of pubs and cafés in Moreton-on-Marsh, Chipping Norton and Stow-on-the-Wold.

Gate Hangs High Inn, Hook Norton
1.5km (1 mile) north of Hook Norton, on the left as you approach the crossroads at direction 5. A Les Routiers sign is displayed and meals are served.

Bell Inn, Hook Norton
Real ale, bar meals and a garden.

Wyatts Farm Shop and Tearooms, Great Rollright
On the right 1km (0.5 miles) after Great Rollright. Coffee, lunches and teas.

Chequers, Churchill
On the left as you pass through the village, serving home-cooked food.

King's Head, Bledington
Morning coffee, real ale, bar snacks and a restaurant.

Route description

From the centre of Moreton-in-Marsh head east along the A44, SP Oxford.

1 TL SP Great Wolford. At this junction is the Three Shire Stone, which originally marked the intersection of boundaries of Gloucestershire, Oxfordshire, Warwickshire and Worcestershire. It now stands on the boundaries of the first three.

2 Arrive Great Wolford. At XR TR SP Little Wolford then TL SP Little Wolford.
6km (3.5 miles)

3 TJ TL onto A3400 SP Shipston and Stratford and almost immediately TR SP Cherington, Stourton and Sutton Brailes.

4 TJ TR SP Whichford, Ascott and Hook Norton. Continue through Whichford and SO at XR. *12km (7.5 miles)*

5 XR TR SP Hook Norton and Swerford. Go through Hook Norton, following SP Chipping Norton. *20km (12.5 miles)*

6 TJ TL SP Great Rollright and Chipping Norton.

7 TJ TR SP Great Rollright and Chipping Norton. Continue along Oxfordshire Cycle Way through Church End and SO across A3400.
24km (15 miles)

8 XR TL SP Little Rollright and Chipping Norton. *30km (18.5 miles)*

9 TR SP Over Norton.

10 At TJ in Over Norton TR SP Chipping Norton.

11 At roundabout as you enter Chipping Norton, bear right SP Town Centre and go down main street. Exit the town on B4450 SP Churchill. *35km (21.5 miles)*

12 Arrive Churchill village. On leaving the village TR SP Kingham and Bledington.
39.5km (24.5 miles)

13 TJ TR SP Bledington. Follow B4450 through Bledington and onwards up Martin's Hill. *43.5km (27 miles)*

14 TJ TL on A436 SP Stow.
50km (31 miles)

15 In Stow, at XR (traffic lights) TR SP Moreton-in-Marsh (on A429).

16 TR SP Broadwell and Evenlode.

17 TJ TR SP Evenlode and Oddington, then TL SP Evenlode and Adlestrop.
54.5 km (34 miles)

18 TJ TL SP Evenlode and Moreton-in-Marsh.

19 TJ TL SP Evesham and ride back into Moreton. *62.5km (39 miles)*

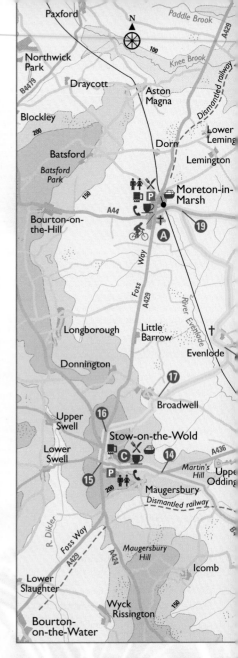

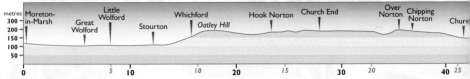

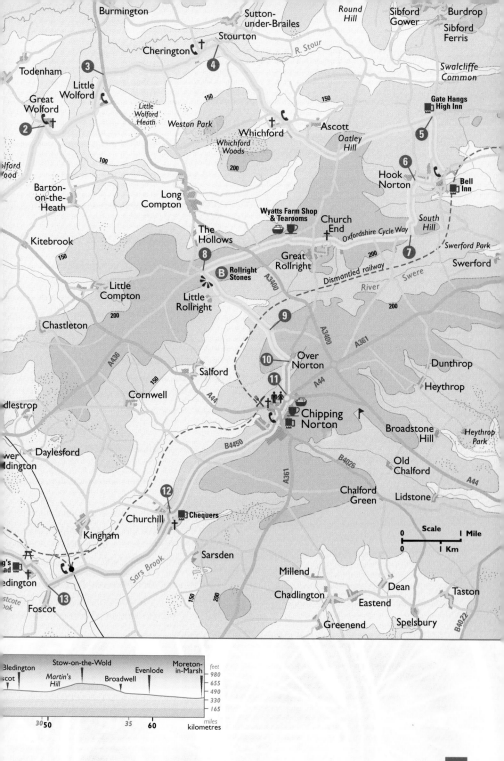

Burmington

Sutton-
under-Brailes

Round
Hill

Sibford
Gower

Burdrop

Sibford
Ferris

Stourton

R. Stour

Cherington

4

Swalcliffe
Common

Todenham

3

Little
Wolford

Gate Hangs
High Inn

Great
Wolford

2

Little
Wolford
Heath

Weston Park

Whichford

Ascott

Oatley
Hill

5

6

Bell
Inn

Whichford
Woods

Barton-
on-the-
Heath

olford
ood

Long
Compton

100

200

Hook
Norton

South
Hill

Swerford Park

Kitebrook

The
Hollows

Wyatts Farm Shop
& Tearooms

Church
End

Oxfordshire Cycle Way

7

Swerford

150

8

B Rollright
Stones

Great
Rollright

A3400

200

Dismantled railway

River Swere

Little
Compton

Chastleton

200

Little
Rollright

9

200

A3400

A361

Dunthrop

Salford

10

Over
Norton

Heythrop

Cornwell

150

A436

A44

11

Broadstone
Hill

Heythrop
Park

dlestrop

Chipping
Norton

Daylesford

ddington

B4450

Old
Chalford

A44

wer
ddington

A361

B4026

Chalford
Green

Lidstone

12

Chequers

Churchill

Kingham

Scale		
0		1 Mile
0		1 Km

Sarsden

g's
ad
edington

Sars Brook

Millend

Dean

Taston

13

Foscot

150

200

Chadlington

Eastend

Spelsbury

B4022

Greenend

Bledington
scot

Stow-on-the-Wold

Martin's
Hill

Broadwell

Evenlode

Moreton-
in-Marsh

feet
980
655
490
330
165

30 50

35

60

miles
kilometres

Route 19
TETBURY AND THE FROME VALLEY

Route information

Distance 63km (39 miles)

Grade Strenuous

Terrain Apart from the return to Tetbury along the A433 and a short section of the A419 in Chalford, this circuit is on unclassified roads, some of them single track. There are several hills, the longest being up to and through Oakridge.

Time to allow 5-6 hours.

Getting there by car Tetbury is south of Stroud on the B4014 and on the A433, south west from Cirencester. There are several car parks in Tetbury.

Getting there by train Kemble is the nearest station, about 14.5km (9 miles) from Tetbury. Telephone (0345) 484950 for information.

From Tetbury, through the Frome Valley to Miserden, along to Woodmancote and Bagendon, returning south west over the wolds to Tetbury. There are places, particularly in the first half of the circuit, where your bike's lower gears will be needed and you may even find yourself walking now and then. Tetbury, a wool town, is well known for its Market House, built in 1665 for the wool trade, and its 18th-century church, St Mary's. The large church windows still contain pieces of medieval glass. Woodmancote and Bagendon are small backwater villages that are not visited as often as some of the better known ones.

Places of interest along the route

Ⓐ Market House, Minchinhampton

Built 1698, this was a market house for wool. The building has connections with Sarah Siddons (1755-1831) the actress who was well-known for her tragic roles. The interior of the house can be seen by appointment only on Saturdays, Sundays and Bank Holidays 0900-1700. Admission free. Telephone (01453) 886904 for information or to make an appointment to visit.

Ⓑ Misarden Park Gardens, Miserden

This country house garden was first planted over 300 years ago and has been developed since then. It contains a rose garden, perennial border, topiary, yew walk, walled garden and woodland trail. Plants are available for sale from the nursery. Open from April to September Tuesday-Thursday, 0930-1630. Charge. Telephone (01285) 821303.

Ⓒ Tetbury Police Museum, Tetbury

The museum is housed in the original cells of the old police station and contains many artefacts from the Gloucestershire Constabulary. Open from March to October Monday-Saturday 1015-1615. Admission free. Telephone (01666) 503552 for further information.

Food and drink

Tetbury has many hotels, pubs and cafés.

Coffee Bean Café, Minchinhampton
On your left as you travel through this small town. Open Tuesday-Friday 1000-1700, Saturday 1000-1230, closed Sunday. Morning coffee, light lunches and teas.

New Red Lion Inn, Chalford
On the right in Chalford, serving real ales and bar snacks.

Stirrup Cup Inn, Bisley
Popular village pub for morning coffee and bar meals.

Carpenters Arms Inn, Miserden
A warm welcome and bar meals at this friendly pub.

Trouble House Inn, near Tetbury
On your right as you cycle down the A433 towards Tetbury. Dating from the 17th century, the pub has a long history, details of which are displayed in the bar. Morning coffee, real ales and bar meals ranging from sandwiches to steaks.

Route description

Leave Tetbury on the B4067, passing the Chipping market square.

1 At XR with A433, SO SP Cherington.

2 Arrive Cherington and TL SP Hampton Fields and Stroud. You will see three roads – take the central one and follow the road downhill to Cherington Pond. *6km (3.5 miles)*

3 At Hampton Fields XR SO SP Minchinhampton.

4 At Minchinhampton XR TR into the High Street. *10km (6 miles)*

5 XR SO into the Knapp. The lane narrows and the surface becomes rough for 200m (220 yards) or so.

6 Take LHF downhill and almost immediately TL down Hyde Hill.

7 After a railway bridge, TJ TR SP Chalford, Brownshill and Bisley. At XR TR SP Village.

8 Take LHF SP Chalford Vale and go along the High Street.

9 TJ TL SP Oakridge and Bisley. Climb to Oakridge and follow SP Bisley.
16km (10 miles)

10 TJ TR SP Cheltenham, Stroud and Birdlip. Then take LHF into Bisley village.

11 Multiple junction by Stirrup Cup Inn. Take the lane SP Unsuitable for Wide Vehicles.
20km (12.5 miles)

12 TJ TR SP The Camp and Birdlip.

13 XR TR SP Miserden. *24km (15 miles)*

14 Take LHF SP Miserden.

15 TR in Miserden, past the Carpenters Arms Inn (30.5km/19 miles). You might, if you wish, be able to cycle through Misarden Park – ask for permission at the plant nursery in the park. If you do this, keep SO into Winstone as you emerge from the park, and join the route at direction 18.

16 XR TL SP Winstone.

17 TJ TL SP Winstone and Cheltenham. Keep on this road into Winstone.

18 TL SP Elkstone and Birdlip then at XR, SO SP Cirencester. *34.5km (21.5 miles)*

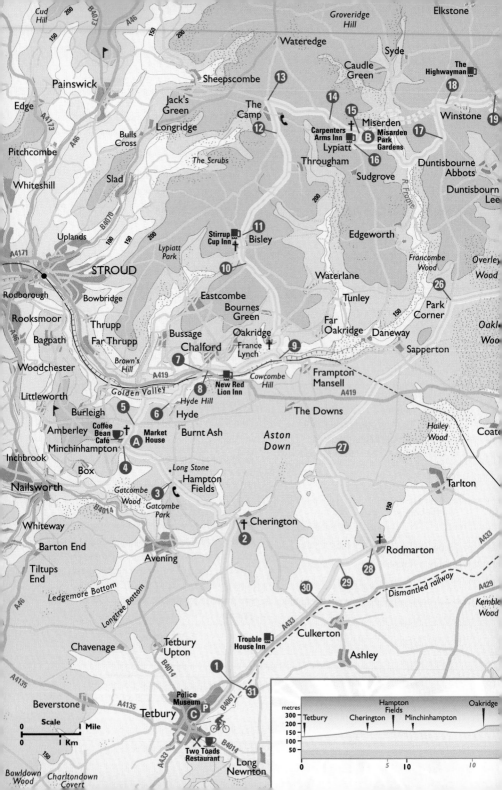

19 At XR with A417, SO SP Woodmancote.

20 TJ TR SP Woodmancote and Cirencester.

21 Take RHF SP Bagendon and Cirencester.
40.5km (25 miles)

22 At Bagendon Church TJ TL (no SP).

23 Arrive Perrott's Brook XR. TR SP Daglingworth and Cirencester.
44km (27.5 miles)

24 SO at A417 XR.

25 At Daglingworth TJ, TR and follow road as it takes a left hand bend by the Village Hall. Then SO at junction SP Sapperton and Stroud.

26 TJ TL SP Sapperton and Stroud. Continue to A419 and SO at XR. *49.5km (31 miles)*

27 XR TL SP Rodmarton and Tarlton.
53.5km (33 miles)

28 At Rodmarton XR TR SP Hazleton and Cherington.

29 TL SP Culkerton and Tetbury.

30 TJ TR onto A433, SP Bath.
58.5km (36.5 miles)

31 TL and return to the centre of Tetbury.
63km (39 miles)

Note – a new trunk road is under construction between Gloucester and Swindon. On completion it will supersede parts of the A417 and affect the route above at directions 19 and 24. At direction 19 the new road will be passed by means of an underpass. At direction 24 the new road will have an underpass to the north of the present junction – after direction 23, take RHF at next junction. TL to the underpass then at TJ TR to Daglingworth.

SOUTHERN COTSWOLD EDGE – NAILSWORTH LOOP

Route information

 Distance 69.5km (43 miles)

Grade Strenuous

Terrain The route mostly follows unclassified roads with a few sections on a cycleway and along A and B roads. The section from Cam to beyond Horton is extremely undulating, justifying the strenuous grading, though none of the hills are major ones. Beyond this there are only two climbs of any consequence; steep but relatively short.

Time to allow 5-7 hours.

Getting there by car Nailsworth is a small town on the A46 between Cheltenham and Bath and about 8km (5 miles) south of Stroud. There is a car park adjacent to Nailsworth bus station, a short distance from the main street.

Getting there by train The nearest railway station is at Stroud on the line between Gloucester and Swindon. Telephone (0345) 484950 for further information.

Down through the Nailsworth valley and into the main Stroudwater valley – the route heads generally south on the lower slopes of the Cotswold escarpment to Horton before climbing to the upper levels of the hills. At

Hawkesbury Upton the route follows a course over the Cotswolds' broad top. After dipping briefly into the upper reaches of the Ozleworth valley at Newington, the route returns to the Nailsworth valley, with a final descent from Horsley to the starting point at Nailsworth.

Places of interest along the route

A **Tyndale's Monument, North Nibley**
William Tyndale was the first man to translate the Bible into English, during the 16th century. His birthplace was believed to have been at North Nibley and a great monument (34m, 111 feet tall) was built on the hill above the village. There is a footpath up to the monument and the tower can be ascended by an internal spiral staircase. A key to the monument can be obtained from Knoyle House (opposite the start of the footpath) or from the Stores, Bars Lane, North Nibley. There is a small charge and an additional deposit is requested for the key. The view is superb even if you do not climb the monument.

B **Wotton-under-Edge Heritage Centre, Wotton-under-Edge**
Wotton was first documented in a Saxon Royal Charter dating from AD940 and in 1252 a Royal Charter was obtained enabling the town to hold a weekly fair and yearly market. Located in a converted fire station in the Chipping (the old market square), the Heritage Centre houses a changing display of artefacts from Wotton's industry and crafts and has many photographs, postcards, documents, maps and books of local

interest. Souvenir shop and tourist information. Open throughout the year: during the summer Tuesday-Saturday 1000-1700; during the winter Tuesday-Saturday 1000-1600. From June to October on the first Sunday in the month 1400-1700. Modest charge. Telephone (01453) 521541.

ⓒ Horton Court, Horton

A National Trust property, Horton Court is a manor house constructed of Cotswold stone, containing a 12th-century Norman hall. Open from April to October, Wednesdays and Saturdays 1400-1800, or dusk if earlier. Charge. Telephone the National Trust Regional Office on (01985) 843600 for further information.

ⓓ Somerset Monument, Hawkesbury Upton

Another landmark on the Cotswold edge, with extensive views. The monument was built in memory of Lord Edward Somerset who fought against the French in the Battle of Waterloo. It can be ascended by a spiral staircase – the key is kept at the house nearby.

ⓔ Ruskin Mill, Nailsworth

The Ruskin Mill is an arts and craft centre with a permanent exhibition of work produced by local craftsmen: stained glass window worker; egg-tempera artist; cabinet maker; architect of ecological buildings; local artists; blacksmith; leather worker; rag-rug maker; photographer; jeweller; and basketmaker. There is also a working waterwheel, an exhibition of reed beds and an organic vegetable shop selling local produce. Exhibition open daily, all year round 1000-1600. Café open all year round, Tuesday-Saturday 1100-1600, Sundays and Bank Holidays 1500-1800. The workshops are open by prior arrangement only. Telephone (01453) 832571.

Food and drink

There are cafés and a number of pubs in Nailsworth and Wotton-under-Edge. Refreshments are also available at the Ruskin Mill in Nailsworth.

🍺 Yew Tree Inn, between Cam and Stinchcombe

The pub stands at a road junction on your right as you approach from Cam after direction 6 – take care as you cross this junction to approach Stinchcombe. Home-cooked meals are available.

🍺 Black Horse Inn, North Nibley

Strategically placed at the top of a climb, you will see the pub on your left as you arrive in the centre of the village. Bar meals available.

🍺 Fox Inn, Hawkesbury Upton

The pub is on the opposite side of the road as you turn into France Lane at direction 14. Bar meals available.

🍺 Royal Oak, Leighterton

Right on the route, serving real ale and bar meals.

🍺 Hunters Hall Inn, Kingscote

The 16th-century Hunters Hall was at one time a coaching inn. Its bars and restaurant have beamed ceilings and the log fires and antique furniture lend an old world atmosphere. There are rumours of hauntings in the pub, and strange things have certainly happened. However, there is nothing odd about the real ale and good food served here.

Route description

Leave Nailsworth car park and bus station at the northern end and go into Spring Lane. After a few metres, TL along the A46 (roundabout) then TR (by Egypt Mill SP). Almost immediately TL into Egypt Mill car park. The cycleway starts in the far corner of the car park.

1 Just beyond the Dudbridge tunnel there is a controlled crossing of the A419 (5.5km/3.5 miles). Go along the cycleway, until you reach a set of traffic lights. Cross the road and continue along the cycleway, at first by the side of the A419, then turning away to the left.

2 At end of cycleway TL and then TR along the canal towpath for 50m (55 yards). Then TL and follow SP Frocester at next junction.

3 TJ TR SP Frocester. **10km (6 miles)**

4 TJ TR SP Cam and Dursley.

5 TJ TL onto A4135 SP Dursley.

6 Near the top of a rise take RHF (B4060) at a roundabout, SP North Nibley and Stinchcombe. **19km (12 miles)**

7 At North Nibley XR SO, SP Wotton and Chipping Sodbury. Just beyond the junction is the start of the footpath to Tyndale's Monument. **24km (15 miles)**

8 Arrive Wotton-under-Edge and descend hill to roundabout (at War Memorial). SO and then almost immediately TR SP Wortley, Alderley and Hillesley.

9 Go through Hillesley village then TR SP Hawkesbury. **31.5km (19.5 miles)**

10 XR (at first sight this looks like a TJ – there is a gate opposite) SO through gate. This is a public road in poor condition.

11 Emerge through a gate by Hawkesbury church. At TJ TR and then almost immediately TL SP Horton. **34.5 km (21.5 miles)**

12 TJ TL and climb the hill.

13 TL SP Hawkesbury Upton and Dunkirk and almost immediately take LHF.

14 TJ TL into France Lane, SP Hillesley and Wotton. **41.5km (26 miles)**

15 TR SP Starveall, or divert SO to the Somerset Monument. Continue to Starveall and cross the A46, with care.

16 At TJ TL along A433, SP Cirencester. **46km (28.5 miles)**

17 Go through Didmarton and TL SP Leighterton.

18 Arrive Leighterton. Passing the Royal Oak, at XR TR SP Westonbirt and Tetbury.

19 XR TL SP Dursley and Wotton-under-Edge. **56km (35 miles)**

20 Cross the A46 and TL SP Newington. Climb ahead, past the deserted church of Newington Bagpath.

21 TJ TR SP Kingscote and Tetbury. **61km (38 miles)**

22 At A4135 TJ TL then TR SP Kingscote. Then at TJ TR and go past church.

23 Arrive at the A46 and immediately TL (no SP).

24 Meet the B4058 at Horsley. At TJ TR towards Nailsworth.

25 Arrive Nailsworth. At TJ TL onto A46, then TL (sharply) and TR into the car park. **69.5 km (43 miles)**

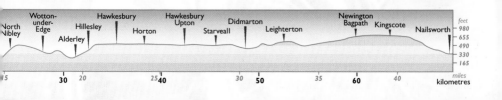

NORTHERN COTSWOLD EDGE – WINCHCOMBE LOOP

Route information

Distance 73km (45.5 miles)

Grade Moderate

Terrain The route is split between unclassified and B roads, with one steep climb.

Time to allow 5-7 hours.

Getting there by car Winchcombe is north of Cheltenham and south of Stratford on the B4632. There are signposted car parks in Winchcombe.

Getting there by train Cheltenham is the nearest station, 16km (10 miles) away, on the main line between Birmingham and Bristol. Telephone (0345) 484950 for information.

From Winchcombe, climbing up Salter's Hill (the line of the ancient Saltway) and then onto Snowshill and Chipping Campden. The route continues north east to Lower Quinton, rounds Meon Hill (the last outpost of the Cotswolds) and then heads south west along the foot of the Cotswold escarpment, back to Winchcombe.

Places of interest along the route

Ⓐ Hailes Abbey, Winchcombe

Hailes Abbey, dedicated in 1251, was built by Henry VIII's brother Richard. It is now a picturesque ruin, run by English Heritage. Museum and gift shop on the site. Open daily from April to the end of September 1000-1300 and 1400-1800; during October 1000-1300 and 1400-1600; from November to March, Wednesday-Sunday 1000-1300 – at this time of year please telephone to confirm opening times on (01242) 602398. Charge.

Ⓑ Snowshill Manor, Snowshill

Owned by the National Trust, Snowshill Manor contains a fascinating collection – from navigation to musical instruments, Samurai armour to bicycles. Gardens, restaurant and gift shop. Open daily (except Tuesday) from April to October 1200-1700; during July and August open every day. Charge. Telephone (01386) 852410.

Ⓒ Broadway Tower Country Park

Exhibition featuring displays on the woollen industry, William Morris (a regular visitor) and the experiences of local people during World War II. There are animal enclosures containing Highland cattle, Cotswold sheep and red deer, adventure playground, picnic and barbecue areas (fuel on sale), and a restaurant. Open daily from April to October 1000-1800. Charge. Telephone (01386) 852390.

Ⓓ Chipping Campden

Chipping Campden is a picturesque north Cotswolds town, containing many beautiful old buildings. The Guild of Handicrafts moved to Chipping Campden from London in 1902 and although it closed in 1908, many of the craftsmen stayed and some of their descendents are still working in the Old Silk Mill.

❺ Hidcote Manor Garden, near Chipping Campden

These beautiful gardens comprise a series of smaller gardens, each with a different theme. National Trust owned. Shop, plant sales and restaurant. There is a tea bar outside Hidcote Manor, for which entrance to the garden is not necessary. Open daily (except Tuesday and Friday) from April to October; daily in June and July (except Friday). From April to September 1100-1800, during October 1100-1700. Charge. Telephone (01386) 438333.

Food and drink

There are numerous pubs and cafés in Winchcombe and Chipping Campden. Refreshments are available at Snowshill Manor, Broadway Tower Country Park, Hidcote Manor Garden and Toddington Rail Centre.

Orchard Tearoom
Adjacent to Hailes Abbey.

Snowshill Arms, Snowshill
Bar meals available.

College Arms, Lower Quinton
Strategically placed at the northern most point of the route. Meals available.

Threeways House, Mickleton
Coffee and home-made biscuits, bar meals and afternoon teas.

Childswickham Inn, Childswickham
On the corner as the route turns left at direction 18. Meals available.

Plaisterers Arms, Winchcombe
Right by the start (and finish) of the route – cyclists and walkers warmly welcomed. Good pub food.

❻ Stanway House, Stanway

A Jacobean manor house with gatehouse, old brewery, Medieval tithe barn, extensive grounds and formal gardens. Open from June to September, Tuesday-Thursday, 1400-1700. Charge. Telephone (01386) 584469.

❼ Gloucestershire & Warwickshire Steam Railway, Toddington Rail Centre

Steam and diesel locomotives run from Toddington to Winchcombe, Gretton and beyond, before returning to Toddington. Special events are held at weekends throughout the year. Picnic area, shop and tearoom at Toddington. Open all year round with variable services, first daily departure around mid-morning, the last in the early evening. Admission to Toddington Station is free but there is a charge for train journeys. Telephone (01242) 621405 for a talking timetable.

Route description

From the central car park in Winchcombe, head north west along the B4632 towards Broadway and Stratford.

1 TR SP Hailes Abbey. After the turning to the Abbey, climb Salter's Hill.

2 TJ TL. Stunning views to the left.
7.5km (5 miles)

3 Cross the B4077, then at XR TL SP Snowshill and Broadway. *12km (7.5 miles)*

4 TL SP Snowshill and Broadway.
16km (10 miles)

5 In Snowshill village TR (sharp) SP Chipping Campden and Bourton. Then, TL SP Broadway Tower and Chipping Campden.

6 XR TL SP Broadway. You will pass the entrance to Broadway Tower Country Park on the left.

7 XR, SO across the A44 SP Saintbury. Picnic site on the left. *21.5km (13.5 miles)*

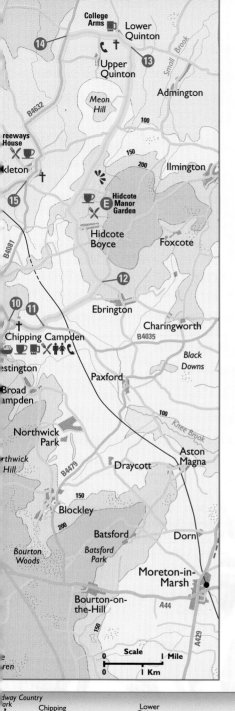

8 XR TR SP Chipping Campden and Mickleton.

9 XR TR SP Chipping Campden. Go into Chipping Campden and along the main street.

25km (15.5 miles)

10 TR (along Cidermill Lane) SP Ebrington and Paxford.

11 TL SP Ebrington.

12 XR TL SP Hidcote and Mickleton and continue past the entrance to Hidcote Manor.

30km (19 miles)

13 TJ TL SP Quinton and Stratford.

37.5 km (23.5 miles)

14 TJ TL onto the B4632 SP Mickleton and Broadway. Continue through Mickleton.

15 XR TR SP Cheltenham and Broadway.

44.5km (28 miles)

16 At roundabout SO SP Childswickham.

51.5km (32 miles)

17 TJ TL onto the A44 then TR SP Childswickham.

18 In Childswickham (by Childswickham Inn) TL SP Buckland. Then at next TJ TL.

55km (34.5 miles)

19 TJ TR SP Cheltenham and Winchcombe.

20 TL SP Stanton. Follow road, keeping right through Stanton, then TL (SP Stanway and Stow-on-the-Wold) to Stanway.

60km (37.5 miles)

21 XR TR SP Tewkesbury and Winchcombe. SO at roundabout.

22 XR TL SP Greet and Winchcombe (68.5km/43 miles). Cycle along the B4078, back to Winchcombe.

73km (45.5 miles)

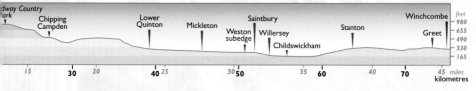

NORTHLEACH, NAUNTON, BROADWELL AND BLEDINGTON

Route information

Distance   74km (46 miles)

Grade   Strenuous

Terrain   Country lanes in the north Cotswolds – the first half of the ride is hilly, although the second part is flatter and easier. There is a small stretch of bridleway on this route.

Time to allow   4-7 hours.

Getting there by car   Northleach is just south of the A40 between Oxford and Cheltenham. Parking is available in the Market Square.

Getting there by train   There are no convenient rail links to the start of this route.

This ride through the north Cotswolds starts in Northleach – like many Cotswold towns and villages, made prosperous throughout the 15th and 16th centuries by the wool trade. The route follows hilly country lanes to Naunton and on to Broadwell, from where it starts to wend its way back through Bledington, the Rissingtons and downhill to Great Barrington, before returning to Northleach. The village greens at Broadwell and Bledington would make good places for a picnic. Adlestrop, at direction 20 on the eastern corner of the route, no longer has a train station, but the station bench sits at the entrance to the village – it is inscribed with a poem you may enjoy reading.

Places of interest along the route

A Northleach Church, Northleach

Northleach Church is considered to be one of the finest Cotswold wool churches – wealthy wool merchants financed its rebuilding during the 15th century. It contains a famous collection of wool merchants' brasses. Open daily throughout the year. Admission free.

B Cotswold Countryside Collection, Northleach

This museum of country life is housed in the remaining buildings of the Northleach House of Correction, built in 1791 and one of the country prisons of Gloucestershire. There is a restored cell block and 19th-century courtroom. The museum contains examples of the crafts and tools necessary to rural life, harvest wagons and other horse-drawn vehicles. There is a history of farming, from prehistoric through to Victorian times and an exhibition recreating a laundry, kitchen and dairy in the days before labour-saving devices. Tearoom and picnic area. Open daily from April to October, Monday-Saturday 1000-1700, Sunday 1400-1700. Charge. Telephone (01451) 860715.

C Keith Harding's World of Mechanical Music, Northleach

Billed as a 'unique experience in sound', this award-winning museum displays all manner of musical boxes, self-playing instruments and clocks, maintained on the premises. Listen to concert performances from Grieg, Rachmaninov and Gershwin; a 1920s Berlin café piano; a 1930s gramophone; and experience a Victorian music room. Guided tours include demonstrations of all types of organs, pianos, musical boxes and gramophones. Gift shop, antique clocks and musical boxes for sale. Open daily all year round (except Christmas Day) 1000-1800. Charge. Telephone (01451) 860181.

Ⓓ Evenlode Church, Evenlode

The village church at Evenlode has one of the few remaining *sanctus* chairs (a place of protection for the persecuted) in the country.

Food and drink

Northleach has a number of hotels and pubs and there is a tearoom at the Cotswold Countryside Collection.

Ⓧ☕ Corner Green Restaurant and Teashop, Northleach

On the right, out of Market Square, opposite Keith Harding's World of Mechanical Music – coffee, lunches and teas.

🍺 Black Horse, Naunton

At direction 8, continue into Naunton. The pub is on the left serving morning coffee (from 1100), real ales and bar snacks.

🍺 The Fox, Broadwell

At the west end of the green in Broadwell. Morning coffee (from 1100), real ales and bar snacks.

🍺 The Plough, Kingham

En route through Kingham – real ales and sandwiches available.

🍺 King's Head, Bledington

On the village green, serving morning coffee (from 1100), real ales and bar snacks.

🍺 New Inn, Nether Westcote

On the right as you go through the village. Real ales and bar snacks available.

🍺 Fox Inn, Little Barrington

By the River Windrush, between Great and Little Barrington, serving coffee (from 1100), real ales and bar snacks.

🍺 Sherborne Arms, Aldsworth

On the B4425, just before you turn into Aldsworth at direction 34. Real ales and bar snacks available.

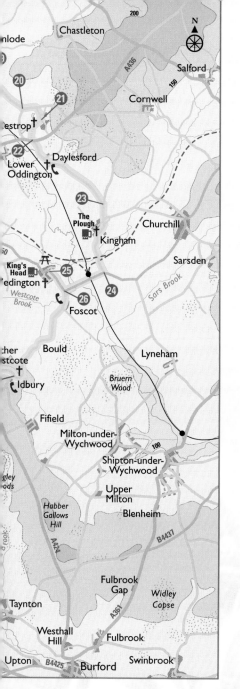

Route description

From Northleach Market Place TR along the High Street.

1 TL out of Northleach SP Farmington, and then go under the A40.

2 TL TJ SP Notgrove. SO across the A429, SP Notgrove. *3.5km (2 miles)*

3 TR TJ SP Notgrove, along a hilly road.

4 TR SP Notgrove and into the village. *9.5km (6 miles)*

5 TJ TR and then TL SP Bourton.

6 SO across A436 SP Aylworth.

7 Arrive B4068 and bear right SP Naunton. *13.5km (8.5 miles)*

8 TL (no SP) and up the hill to Grange Hill Farm. At TJ (no SP) TL.

9 TR TJ SP Lower Swell and continue uphill. *17.5km (11 miles)*

10 SO at XR (no SP) across open countryside and then downhill.

11 TL SP Condicote then SO at XR with B4077.

12 SP Condicote TL into the village. *22.5km (14 miles)*

13 In Condicote TR at walled village green and then TR SP Stow-on-the-Wold.

14 TL TJ SP Stow-on-the-Wold.

15 SO SP Stow then TR at A424 SP Stow. *26.5km (16.5 miles)*

16 TL SP Donnington TL.

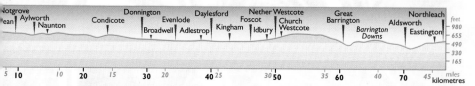

17 SO across A429 SP Broadwell and into the village.

18 TL SP Evenlode. *32.5km (20 miles)*

19 TL into Evenlode. Then return along the same road to junction and bear left.

20 SP Adlestrop TL; TR into Adlestrop; TR SP To our Church.

21 Follow SP Bridlepath and go down slope, through gate and across field. *37km (23 miles)*

22 SO at A436 SP Kingham.

23 TR TJ SP Kingham.

24 TR at B4450 TJ SP Bledington and continue to the village green. *43.5km (27 miles)*

25 Return along B4450.

26 TR SP Idbury – a climb ahead to the village. *47.5km (29.5 miles)*

27 TR SP Westcote.

28 TL (no SP) just after church.

29 At A424 TR SP Stow. TL SP Little Rissington. *50.5km (31.5 miles)*

30 TL at XR SP the Barringtons and go downhill to Great Barrington. *58.5km (36.5 miles)*

31 SO SP Little Barrington.

32 Arrive A40 and go SO (with care).

33 TR at B4425 SP Aldsworth.

34 TR SP Aldsworth and go into the village *67.5km (42 miles)*

35 TL SP Northleach.

36 TL TJ SP Northleach, returning to the start of the route. *74km (46 miles)*

Northleach Church

Route information

Distance 76.5km (48 miles)

Grade Strenuous

Terrain Almost all unclassified and narrow lanes, with short stretches along A and B roads. There are a number of hills to be negotiated, particularly in the first half of the ride. However, the later stages are comparatively flat. There is an alternative off-road section, which adds around 12.5 km (8 miles) to the total distance – it is strenuous and a mountain bike is necessary.

Time to allow 5-8 hours. Following the off-road section will add around two hours to the riding time.

Getting there by car Kemble is on the A429 between Cirencester and Chippenham, about 8km (5 miles) south west of Cirencester. There is a large car park at the railway station (charge for parking).

Getting there by train Kemble Station is on the line between Gloucester and Swindon and all trains stop there. Telephone (0345) 484950 for information.

From Kemble, south to Elkstone, and the alternative off-road section. The route wends its way east and south east, past Chedworth to Bibury and Coln St. Aldwyns, before returning to Kemble. During the ride the River Frome is crossed twice; the middle section of the ride follows the valley of the River Coln (a tributary of the Thames); and towards the end of the ride the headwaters of the Thames itself are bridged. The route passes through many attractive Cotswold villages, particularly Arlington and Bibury, but they can get very crowded on a fine summer's day.

Places of interest along the route

Ⓐ Source of the River Thames (Thameshead)
The source of the River Thames can be reached by a footpath that starts beside the railway, beyond the Thameshead Inn. The spring is about 800m (0.5 mile) from the A433, but in a dry spell not a drop of water is to be seen.

Ⓑ Thames and Severn Canal Tunnel
When the two mile long tunnel was completed in 1789 it was the longest tunnel in the world and regarded as a wonder of engineering. The tunnel was blocked by a rockfall in 1916 and has not been used as a through route since. There are sometimes boat trips into the tunnel from the southern end, although not in high summer due to low water levels. The southern end of the tunnel can be reached by a rough road, 400m from the lane. The northern end of the tunnel was recently restored to its original castellated appearance and can be reached by a 400m walk from the Daneway Inn.

Ⓒ Chedworth Roman Villa, Yanworth
This National Trust property is one of the best Romano British villas in Britain. It was, in fact,

a Roman country mansion and outbuildings, situated in a sheltered valley. The lower parts of many of the buildings have been exposed and there is plenty to see including a water shrine and spring, two bath houses and fine 4th-century mosaics. An on-site museum explains the history of the villa. Open from March to October, Tuesday-Sunday and Bank Holidays 1000-1700; during November, Tuesday-Sunday 1000-1600. Charge. Telephone (01242) 890256.

D Bibury and Arlington

The River Coln is a prominent feature of Bibury and its close neighbour, Arlington. Bibury was once described by William Morris as 'the most beautiful village in England' and is always popular with visitors (sometimes becoming extremely busy). The much-photographed Arlington Row is owned by the National Trust and is a row of tiny 17th-century cottages that once housed the village weavers. Across from Arlington Row is Rack Isle (also National Trust owned) where the woven cloth was dried. Arlington Mill, once a corn mill, is now a folk museum. The Domesday Book shows that there was a mill here as long ago as 1068. The present mill dates from the 17th century and contains a gallery, exhibitions on the countryside, Victorian life, William Morris and furniture made by members of the Arts and Crafts Movement, who drew inspiration from Morris. The mill grindstones and machinery are still operating. Tea room with a terrace on the mill stream. Gift shop. Open daily from Easter to Christmas 1000-1800. Charge. Telephone (01285) 740368.

E Bibury Trout Farm

Bibury Trout Farm was founded in 1902 and is one of the oldest trout farms in the country. It covers an area of 3 hectares (8 acres) and contains over 40 rearing ponds. The farm produces over ten million rainbow trout eggs and one million fry each year; over 250,000 trout are reared each year. You can feed the trout and gain an insight into the workings of the farm and fish culture. There is a fish counter and delicatessen where you can buy smoked trout, fillets and paté, and locally produced delicacies.

Food and drink

Refreshments are available at Arlington Mill and Bibury Trout Farm

Tunnel House Inn, Tarlton
Adjacent to the southern entrance of the Thames and Severn Canal Tunnel, serving morning coffee and bar meals.

Daneway Inn, Daneway
Near the northern entrance of the tunnel. Morning coffee and meals available.

Mill Inn, Withington
On your left in the village street.

Fossebridge Inn, Fossebridge
Restaurant and bar meals available.

Jenny Wren Tearooms, Bibury
Coffee, lunches and cream teas.

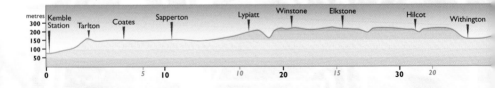

Route description

Leave Kemble Station car park and in the lane TL and go under a railway bridge.

1 At Tarlton village XR TR SP Coates and Cirencester.

2 TJ TL. **5.5km (3.5 miles)**

3 TJ TL onto A419 then take RHF SP Sapperton and Edgeworth.

4 TJ TR SP Edgeworth and Miserden. Start of footpath to canal tunnel on the right.

5 XR TR SP Winstone. **16.5km (10.5 miles)**

6 TJ TL SP Winstone and Cheltenham.

7 In Winstone LHF SP Elkstone and Birdlip then XR TL SP Elkstone and Birdlip. Continue to direction 8 or for the off-road section:
21km (13 miles)

a Approach top of hill, at XR TR into Elkstone village.

b TR SP Public Path and cycle down track.

c TJ TR onto road.

d At junction, TL SP Colesbourne and Cheltenham.

e After sharp right bend continue SO.

f TR at A435. Immediately after Colesbourne Inn TL down no through road and continue through gate and up into field.

g TR through gate then TL through another gate following Bridlepath signs. SO, through gate and then TL at gate and SO through the last gate.

h SO at junction with road.

i Where track splits, take RHF then at cottage TL.

j At junction with road, TL and keep right at next junction.

k TR onto bridleway, SP Wistley Hill. At next bridleway sign, keep right and go SO through gate onto track.

l Through gate TL onto road.

m 18m (20 yards) before junction with A436 note car park for Kilkenny viewpoint. TR at A436 SP Stow.

n TR opposite Kilkenny Inn, down no through road, then TR through gate onto bridleway. Continue uphill through three more gates.

o Immediately before gate TL and go uphill through gate with footpath sign only. Proceed through two more gates.

p Through gate, keep left and at bridleway junction TR and carry SO.

q TJ with road, TL.

r Keep left SP Withington and Chedworth.

s SO SP Andoversford and Cheltenham and continue the route at direction 10.

8 TL at TJ onto A435 SP Cheltenham. After 500m XR TR SP Upper Coberley (26.5km/16.5 miles).

9 After a steep descent, XR SO SP Withington. Keep left at next two junctions. Steep climb follows. **30km (18.5 miles)**

10 Entering Withington, TJ TR SP Roman Villa and Compton Abdale. TR SP Roman Villa and Yanworth. **34.5km (21.5 miles)**

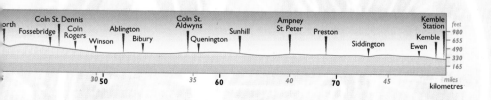

11 TJ TL SP Yanworth and Northleach. TR for Chedworth Roman Villa.

12 TR SP Fossebridge and Cirencester. Continue towards the A429.   **40km (25 miles)**

13 TJ TL onto A429 then TR SP Coln St. Dennis and Bibury.

14 TJ TR (to the right of Coln St. Dennis church) SP Coln Rogers and Bibury. Follow signs to Bibury.   **44km (27.5 miles)**

15 Arrive Bibury and at TJ TL onto B4425. After 600m TR SP Coln St. Aldwyns.   **50.5km (31.5 miles)**

16 TJ TR SP Coln St. Aldwyns and Fairford. At Quenington, XR TR SP Ampney St. Peter and Cirencester. Proceed through Sunhill to A417.   **56km (35 miles)**

17 TJ TR onto A417 SP Cirencester (62.5km/39 miles). TL SP Harnhill and Driffield.

18 At XR take second right.

19 Entering Preston, TJ TL SP Preston and South Cerney.   **67km (41.5 miles)**

20 TR SP Siddington.

21 TJ TL SP Somerford Keynes and Oaksey, then TR SP Ewen and Kemble.   **70.5 km (44 miles)**

22 At Ewen TJ TR SP Kemble and Tarlton. Ride to Kemble village, cross the A429 and take second left back to station car park.   **76.5km (48 miles)**

Note – a new trunk road is under construction between Gloucester and Swindon. It will bypass Cirencester and supersede parts of the A417 and A419. Route 23 will be affected between directions 7 and 8, and 18 and 19. When the new road is complete (after direction 7) TR to go under bridge; the lane between directions 18 and 19 will be closed to vehicular traffic but there will be a pedestrian bridge over the new road that can be used by cyclists.

Route information

Distance 80.5km (50 miles)

Grade Strenuous

Terrain Country lanes and short stretches along A and B roads and a cycleway. This is a hilly route.

Time to allow 5-7 hours.

Getting there by car Stroud is 8km (5 miles) east of the M5. It is approached from the east by the A419 and from the north and south by the A46. The ride starts from Stroud railway station where there is car parking.

Getting there by train Stroud railway station is on the line between Gloucester and Swindon. Telephone (0345) 484950 for information.

From Stroud up onto the Cotswolds to Birdlip, from where there is a wonderful view over the vale. Then over hilly countryside to Sapperton and along relatively unknown lanes to Cherington and Chavenage. Through the lovely Kingscote valley to another viewpoint at Coaley Peak, with views over the River Severn to the Welsh mountains. The route then passes Hetty Pegler's Tump and Uley Bury – two ancient sites – and turns down through Uley and Coaley and back to Stroud.

Places of interest along the route

Ⓐ Barrow Wake, near Birdlip
Panoramic views over the Severn Vale and a good place to picnic. Topograph (3-D model of the surrounding landscape). Always open, free admission.

Ⓑ Sapperton Churchyard, Sapperton
Sapperton was the home and work place of several members of the Cotswold Arts and Crafts movement during the early 19th century. Gimson and the Barnsley brothers are buried in the churchyard.

Ⓒ Chavenage House, Chavenage
Chavenage House is an Elizabethan manor house, built in 1576. It contains tapestry rooms, furniture and relics of the Cromwellian period. The house has been used many times as a location for television productions. Each July the gardens provide the setting for a Shakespearean play and pre-performance picnics. The house is open to the public on Easter Sunday and Easter Monday, and every Thursday and Sunday, from May to September 1400-1700. Charge. Telephone (01666) 502329. Chavenage House (01666 502329).

Ⓓ Coaley Peak, near Nympsfield
Five hectares (12 acres) of grassland with panoramic views over the Severn Vale. It adjoins a National Trust nature reserve where there is a topograph. Always open, free admission.

E Hetty Pegler's Tump (Uley Barrow), near Uley

A chambered long barrow dating from around 2800BC. Hetty Pegler's Tump was a stone age burial place; when it was opened in the 19th century, some 30 skeletons were discovered. You will need a torch to see inside. Open daily, all year round – if the exterior wooden door is locked you can get the key from a cottage on the right along the road towards Uley. Admission free.

F Uley Bury, near Uley

A prehistoric hill fort which could have housed between 2000 and 3000 people. The fort is surrounded by two banks and ditches. Roman coins and pottery have been found on the site. Always open, admission free.

Food and drink

Central Stroud has several pubs and cafés.

Mills Café, Witheys Yard, High Street, Stroud

TL just after the Subscription Rooms and on foot (against a one-way road) walk to the pedestrianised area and TJ at pedestrianised High Street. Witheys Yard is almost opposite. Morning coffee, lunches and teas.

Bear Inn, Bisley

On the right on the route into Bisley, serving morning coffee (from 1100), real ales and bar snacks.

Stirrup Cup, Bisley

En route in Bisley. Morning coffee (from 1100), real ales and bar snacks available.

Fostons Ash Inn, Camp

On the right as you TR onto the B4070. Morning coffee (from 1100), real ales and bar snacks.

Royal George Hotel, Birdlip

On the left just after you TR into Birdlip. Morning coffee (from 1100) and bar snacks served.

Bell Inn, Sapperton

In the village, serving morning coffee (1100), real ales and bar snacks.

Hunters Hall Inn, Kingscote

On the A4135 – at direction 22 keep left instead of SO along road signed The Windmill. Real ales and bar snacks.

Rose and Crown Inn, Nympsfield

On left in the village. Real ales and bar snacks available.

Old Crown Inn, Uley

At the top of the village, on the left, serving real ales and bar snacks.

Fox and Hounds, Coaley

On the route – real ales and bar snacks.

Royal George Hotel, Frocester

To the left of the XR in Frocester. Morning coffee (from 1100), real ales and bar snacks.

View over Severn Vale from Coaley Peak

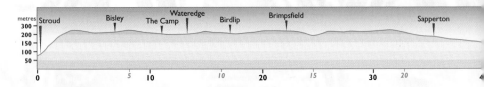

Route description

TL out of Stroud Station and immediately TR around the one-way system. Pass the Subscription Rooms on the left and the clock (in middle of road) on the right and continue to mini roundabout.

1 TL at mini roundabout, SP Bisley. Continue up this road for 6.5km (4 miles) to Bisley village. **_7km (4.5 miles)_**

2 In Bisley TL at TJ opposite shop. Continue through The Camp to the B4070. **_13km (8 miles)_**

3 TR at TJ onto B4070.

4 TR at TJ SP Cheltenham and follow B road sharp left.

5 TL SP Shab Hill to Barrow Wake. **_17.5km (11 miles)_**

6 Return to road and TR. SP Brimpsfield, TL.

7 TR SP Brimpsfield – steep downhill ride here. **_24km (15 miles)_**

8 SO SP Winstone and up a long hill.

9 TR at Gaskill's Farm TJ (no SP). **_31km (19.5 miles)_**

10 SO SP Sapperton.

11 TR SP Sapperton and into the village. **_34.5km (21.5 miles)_**

12 TL SP Kemble, then TR SP Cherington.

13 Arrive A419 XR, SO SP Cherington.

14 SO SP Cherington.

15 TR at TJ SP Tetbury into Cherington (41.5km/26 miles). In Cherington SO, SP Tetbury.

Sapperton Church

16 TR SP Avening.

17 SO SP Chavenage.

18 Arrive B4014. SO SP Chavenage House. **_46.5km (29 miles)_**

19 TR TJ (no SP) – TL for diversion to Chavenage House.

20 Arrive A46 XR and SO (no SP) along Hazlecote Farm Lane and past the farm itself.

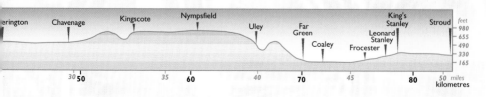

21 TL at junction (no SP) and continue to Kingscote. **53km (33 miles)**

22 In Kingscote SO SP The Windmill.

23 TR at TJ (no SP).

24 At B4058 TJ, TR SP Frocester.

25 TL SP Nympsfield.

26 TR SP Nympsfield, into the village.

27 In Nympsfield SO SP Selsley.

28 B4066 TJ TL and then TR to Coaley Peak. **59km (36.5 miles)**

29 TR out of Coaley Peak along B4066 towards Uley, down Crawley Hill (steep descent) and into Uley. **63.5km (39.5 miles)**

30 TR (no SP) just before Court House and to right of road SP Footway.

31 TR TJ SP Coaley.

32 SO TJ SP Coaley. **69.5km (43 miles)**

33 TR SP Frocester.

34 XR SP Leonard Stanley SO. **74.5km (46.5 miles)**

35 As the road bends right into King's Stanley, TL along Brockley Road. TL TJ at end of Brockley Road.

36 At traffic lights TR then filter left onto cycleway and go SO.

37 At pedestrian crossing, leave cycleway and TL at roundabout. TL and walk along footway to canal path.

38 TR along canal path, and walk for 1.5km (1 mile) to gateway onto tarmac and to A46.

39 At A46 SO and then under subway.

40 For trains to Cheltenham TR up Cheapside after the Bell Hotel. For trains to London SO at roundabout and up Rowcroft under railway bridge; dismount at top, cross road and TR into station. **80.5km (50 miles)**

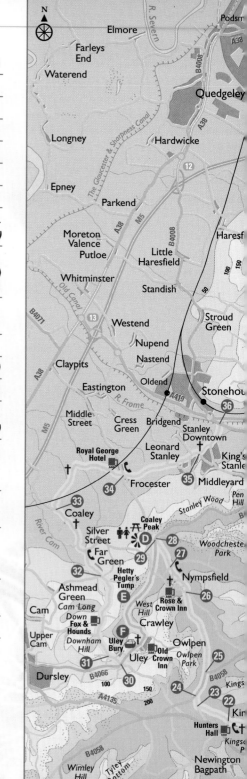

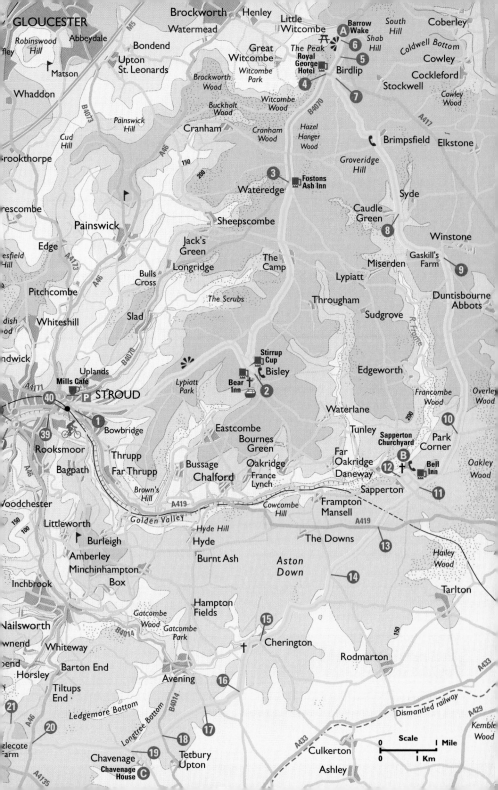

Route information

Distance 100km (62.5 miles)

Grade Strenuous

Terrain A mix of steep hills and gently undulating countryside, mainly on quiet lanes. There is an alternative off-road section in the route, for which a mountain bike would be needed.

Time to allow 6-10 hours. Following the off-road section would add around an hour to the overall time.

Getting there by car Cheltenham is close to the M5 and A40, north of Stroud and Cirencester. The ride starts at the Bath Terrace/Commercial Road car park to the west of Bath Road in Cheltenham.

Getting there by train Cheltenham is on the Paddington-Swindon-Cheltenham line, and also on the line from Worcester. Telephone (0345) 484950 for information. To join the start of the route, leave the station and TR along Queens Road. At the big roundabout SO into Andover Road and immediately right into St Stephens Road. At end of St Stephens Road TR and around The Park. Take third right into Moorend Park Road and up to the traffic lights. SO into Moorend Park Road then Moorend Road. At TJ TR and continue along Leckhampton Road and up the hill to direction 1.

A grande randonnée through some of the Cotswolds' most delightful villages. From Cheltenham, described as the gateway to the Cotswolds, the route heads south to Daglingworth and then east to Netherton. The route joins the Welsh Way (along which Welsh sheep drovers shepherded their flocks to the London markets). The route then heads north to the Slaughters before turning west, with a final steep descent into Cheltenham.

Places of interest along the route

A Cheltenham
This Regency Spa town has beautiful buildings, tree-lined avenues, parks and gardens with superb flower beds, fountains and publi[c] spaces. There is an art gallery, museum an[d] theatre, and the town holds internationa[l] festivals of music and literature. In 177[?] Cheltenham was virtually just a single mai[n] street. The discovery of medicinal spa water[s] changed all this: the Duke of Wellington an[d] King George III were among the notabl[e] visitors. By 1800 Cheltenham's population ha[d] quadrupled and by the late 1920s the town ha[d] a population of over 60,000. Today, the town i[s] still smart, fashionable and prosperous.

B Seven Springs
The headwaters of the River Churn, a tributary o[f] the Thames, are located in the hollow opposit[e] the Seven Springs Inn. Always accessible.

C Daglingworth Church

This lovely church has four Saxon wall sculptures, so smooth they look modern. Note the tiny windows in the vestry wall. There are also interesting brass tablets in the floor of the porch. Usually open. Admission free.

D Barnsley House Gardens, Barnsley

Magnificent gardens owned and developed by Rosemary Verey, the well-known writer on English gardens. They feature spring bulbs and autumn colour, mixed borders, climbing and wall shrubs, vegetable, knot and herb gardens, a Laburnum walk, 18th-century summer houses and a decorative vegetable potager. Open Monday, Wednesday, Thursday and Saturday throughout the year 1000-1800. Charge. Telephone (01285) 740281.

E Old Mill, Lower Slaughter

A mill museum with working water wheel and craft displays. Gift shop and antiques for sale. Refreshments available. Open daily all year round 1000-1800. Charge. Telephone (01451) 820052.

Food and drink

There are numerous pubs, teashops and hotels in the centre of Cheltenham.

Seven Springs Inn, Seven Springs
Opposite the spring. Morning coffee (from 1100), real ales and a restaurant.

Green Dragon Inn, Cockleford
TL in Cowley just after the Manor (after direction 7). The pub is 1km (0.5 miles) along this road. Morning coffee (from 1100), real ales and bar snacks.

The Bear, Perrott's Brook
To the right as you cross the A435. Morning coffee (from 1100), real ales and bar snacks available.

The Village Pub, Barnsley
On B4425 in Barnsley; serving morning coffee (from 1100), real ales and bar snacks.

New Inn, Coln St. Aldwyns
En route, in the village. Bar snacks available.

Fox Inn, Little Barrington
By the River Windrush between Little and Great Barrington. Morning coffee (from 1100), real ales and bar snacks served.

Washbourne Court Hotel, Lower Slaughter
Close to the bridge in the village; serving morning coffee, lunches and teas.

Farmers Arms, Guiting Power
In the centre of the village. Real ales and bar snacks available.

Craven Arms, Brockhampton
Just over the XR in Brockhampton and TL. Morning coffee (from 1100), real ales and bar snacks available.

Route description

Follow the signs out of the car park into Upper Bath Street. TR up Bath Road. Bear left at roundabout opposite Norwood Arms, up Leckhampton Road and on up the hill.
4km (2.5 miles)

1 On a flattish section TL (no SP but on left SP Gates).

2 TJ – dismount and walk along pavement. TR to Seven Springs and then return to A435.
7km (4.5 miles)

3 A435 SP Cirencester TR.

4 TL SP Upper Coberley.

5 TR (no SP).

6 At A435 XR SO SP Cowley. Continue to Cowley.
11.5km (7 miles)

7 TL (no SP) just before Cross Cottage.

8 At A417 XR SO SP Brimpsfield, and continue to Brimpsfield.
15km (9.5 miles)

9 TL TJ SP Caudle Green.

10 SO SP Winstone.
20km (12.5 miles)

11 At Gaskill's Farm TJ TR (no SP).

12 TL SP Daglingworth, then TR.

13 TL SP Daglingworth into the village (26.5km/16.5 miles). At Daglingworth XR, TR to visit church and return. SO SP Perrott's Brook and up a short hill.

14 At A417 SO SP Perrott's Brook.

15 Arrive A435, SO SP Barnsley (31.5km/19.5 miles). SO at XR SP Barnsley.

16 At A429 SO SP Barnsley into Sheephouse Lane, the ancient Welsh Way.

17 TL (no SP) and continue along Welsh Way to Barnsley.
36.5km (22.5 miles,

18 In Barnsley TL along B4425 towards Bibury.

19 TR SP Ready Token.
40km (25 miles)

20 TL at TJ to Ready Token, then SO SP Quenington along Akeman Street (a Roman road).

21 At XR TL SP Coln St. Aldwyns, and go down to the river.
45.5km (28.5 miles,

22 At Coln St. Aldwyns XR TR SP Hatherop, and go down over the river again.

23 Hatherop TJ TL SP Westwell.
51km (31.5 miles

24 TL TJ (no SP).

25 XR SP Barringtons TL.
55km (34 miles

26 At B4425 XR SO SP Barringtons.

27 At A40 XR SO SP Barringtons into Little Barrington.

28 In Little Barrington SO and over stream.
58.5km (36.5 miles

29 In Great Barrington SO SP Little Rissington – long uphill ride ahead.
66km (41 miles

30 TL SP Wyck Rissington – steep downhill here.

31 A429 TL (with care) and TR SP Slaughters.
71km (44 miles

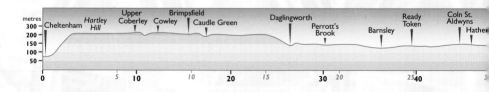

32 TL SP Upper Slaughter. Continue on-road route at direction 33. To follow off-road section take first left after bridge in Upper Slaughter and go uphill to TJ SO onto bridleway then:

a At junction with road, SO. Follow bridleway through gate, TL and continue through two more gates.

b TR at bridleway junction, over a stream and uphill. TR through farm (note it is easy to TL here). Go across field – caution, steep downhill.

c At the end of a wood, SO through gate and across field. TL through next gate and ride downhill, through a gate with only a footpath sign. Continue through another gate then take the lower of the two gates.

d At junction with road TL then TR onto Windrush Way. Keep left across field. Go through three more gates.

e TR over stream and ride diagonally to the left uphill. Before gate TL downhill – caution, very steep. SO through gate and TR in front of next gate, following track.

f TR at road junction and immediately TL onto Windrush Way. TL in front of house and go down through gate. TR before buildings.

g Through gate and turn diagonally right, staying on lower track. SO through five more gates.

h At TJ with A436 TR, taking care on fast road. After B4068 junction, TR (no SP).

i XR TR SP Hawling. Keep left through village and join route at direction 39.

33 TL at B4068.

34 TR XR SP The Quarry.

35 TL SP Guiting Power.

36 TL at TJ SP Guiting Power then TR at TJ SP Guiting Power.

37 TL SP Guiting Power, and go up into the village. *79.5km (49.5 miles)*

38 In Guiting Power TL at Watsons Bakers. Continue along this quiet lane to Hawling. *84.5km (52.5 miles)*

39 TL TJ SP Andoversford.

40 TR XR SP Brockhampton.

41 At junction SP Brockhampton TR. *88km (54.5 miles)*

42 In centre of Brockhampton TL at XR opposite telephone box (no SP).

43 In Sevenhampton TR and cross ford. TL at TJ.

44 At TJ SP Whittington TR. *91.5km (57 miles)*

45 In Whittington SO SP Ham and continue down Ham Hill – caution steep hill.

46 In Ham SO SP Charlton Kings, and into Glenfall Way. *97km (60.5 miles)*

47 Arrive A40 TJ. TR and then first left, opposite garage, into School Road.

48 TR into Lyefield Road and SO at traffic lights into Moorend Road.

49 TR into The Avenue, and take sharp right down path. At end TR along Old Bath Road.

50 TL into Naunton Park Road, then TL at TJ.

51 TR along Naunton Crescent; TR into Exmouth Street; TR into Bath Road; and TL into car park. *100km (62 miles)*

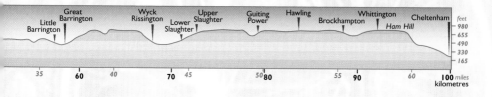

THE CYCLISTS' TOURING CLUB

The CTC is Britain's largest national cycling organisation. Founded in 1878, the CTC has over 40,000 members throughout the UK and overseas, around 200 local groups and 200 independent affiliated clubs. The CTC provides essential services for all leisure cyclists, whether you ride on- or off-road, and works to promote cycling and protect cyclists' interests.

CTC membership makes day-to-day cycling easier. An expert cycling engineer will answer your technical queries about cycle buying, maintenance and equipment. If you get ambitious about your cycling, the CTC's Touring Department has reams of information about cycling anywhere from Avon to Zimbabwe. The shop sells a wide variety of clothing, accessories, books, maps and guide books. The handbook lists practically everything a cyclist could wish to know.

Cycling is one of the healthiest activities there is – it raises your metabolism, burns fat and tones muscle. However, accidents do happen, and the CTC's services mean that when you ride, you are protected by free third party liability of up to £1 million, and by our legal assistance to pursue civil claims.

Club members also receive *Cycle Touring and Campaigning* magazine free six times a year. CT&C regards independent journalism as a service to CTC members. With reports on cycle trips all over the globe, forensic tests on bikes and equipment, and the most vigorous and effective pro-bike campaigning stance anywhere, CT&C is required reading for any cyclist.

The CTC works on behalf of all Britain's 20 million cycle owners. It is lobbying for lower speed limits on country lanes; campaigning so that you can carry bikes on trains; working with local authorities to make towns more cycle-friendly, to ensure that roads are designed to meet cyclists' needs and kept well maintained; making sure that bridleways are kept open; and negotiating cyclists' access to canal towpaths.

Don't be put off by the word 'touring' in the title. Mountain bikers, Sunday potterers, bicycle commuters, families on a day out – cycling is easier and safer with the CTC's knowledge and services in your saddlebag. You will be protecting and informing yourself, and strengthening the campaign for cyclists' rights, on- and off-road.

For further information contact:
Cyclists' Touring Club
Cotterell House
69 Meadrow
Godalming
Surrey
GU7 3HS

Telephone (01483) 417217
Fax (01483) 426994
e-mail: cycling@ctc.org.uk
Web page: http://www.ctc.org.uk